Divine
Encounters...

Melissa Giomi

Melissa Giomi
Facebook: @MelissaGiomiauthor
Instagram: @melissa.giomi

First Paperback Edition August 2022

ISBN 979-8-218-03354-5 (paperback)
ISBN 979-8-218-03353-8 (ebook)

Library of Congress Control Number: 2022913458

Edited by Pia Edberg, piaedberg.com
Blurb by Book Blurb Magic, IG: @bookblurbmagic
Cover & interior design by Karolina Wudniak, karolinawudniak.com

Divine Encounters...

Table of Contents

...in nature

...in chaos

...at the Feast

Introduction

I'm delighted that you picked up my book! It is the culmination of over ten years of writing. After receiving encouragement from family and friends, I decided to take the plunge and write a book!

Putting myself out there is frightening, but I deeply desire to share the beautiful things I have experienced on my journey with Jesus. There have been exciting, joy-filled times, interspersed with sadness, fear, and a long battle with breast cancer. I discovered that there is always hope and the Divine is all around us.

I whole-heartedly believe beauty and joy can be found in an ordinary day. There is peace, and restoration in the ancient rhythms of nature, and deep healing in the chaos of this life we have been given. As you journey with me, I hope that you will find exactly what you need and be richly blessed. Peace be with you and thank you for reading my book.

...in ordinary life

Just a Morning

SUNLIGHT filters through the blinds; the breeze is cool and refreshing through the slightly open bedroom window.

Shifting from dreamy sleep to wakefulness, content and peace-filled. Thank you, Lord, for waking me up—I'm coming!

Cozy cat stirs and stretches, stomping on body parts still under the covers. Time to get up. He knows the routine well.

The scent of brewing coffee brings homey memories to mind; rich and earthy, there is safety in predictability.

Dogs wait politely, then bound outdoors, enjoying freedom after a long, snug night. Noses to the ground on high alert; sniffing out the offending evening invaders; dewdrops spot their muzzles; glinting as the sun peeks through treetops.

Sounds of the morning!

Wind chimes sing softly and gently as the breeze tosses itself about; birds up since dawn cling to the feeders, calling and scolding and jostling for position. Bright reds and yellows, muted greys and black.

The gentle light of early morning gives way to something stronger; fortifying, brighter, life-giving.

Coffee and the Bible sit on the pine table; steam swirls and pages flutter, beckoning and calling. My heart stirs. There are mysteries to unravel here, richness to take in, and understanding waiting to be found. Revelation, peace, and contentment are what I seek—warmth, depth, and life.

Who knows what will come as the day unfolds? Joy? Laughter? Tears? For now, I sit at my Father's feet, listening to Him speak with all my senses, sipping the warm richness of my coffee. It's just a morning on an ordinary day, but it is my joy.

What Are You Seeking?

JOHN 1:38A says, "Jesus turned and saw them following and said to them, 'What are you seeking?'"

When was the last time someone asked you what you wanted, besides the barista in your favorite coffee shop? I mean really asked and wanted to hear the answer. Close your eyes and picture Jesus sitting across from you, asking, "[Your Name], what are you seeking?"

How would you answer Him? Would you, in a panic, try to use your arsenal of Christianese to impress Him with a lofty, holy, righteous answer? Would your mind go blank because you aren't sure what you are seeking? Maybe you blurt out, "I'm seeking You, Lord!" But are you really?

We may wish that He was always our deepest desire, but if we are completely honest, sometimes He isn't. He is not impressed or fooled when we answer Him with what we think He wants to hear.

Jesus can handle our honesty because He already knows the real, nitty-gritty answer.

What are you seeking? Is it to feel safe? Accepted? Do you want to be known and seen? Are you seeking rest because life is hard, and you are worn down? Are you seeking a soulmate or a good friend? Healing? These are all good things to seek, human things that humans crave. Jesus knows this and doesn't reject us for wanting them. He uses worldly, human desires to bring to us what He knows we seek most. Him. Even if you don't know it, feel, or believe it, it has always been Him. In Jesus, the void is filled. In Jesus, we find meaning and value, safety and rest, healing, joy and peace, a best friend, and an eternal soulmate.

So, what is it you are seeking? What does your soul crave? Tell Him and trust Him with the desires of your heart. Whatever it is that your heart and soul seek will ultimately be found in Jesus. Always. He is enough.

He Is Speaking

HAVE YOU HEARD the phrase, "God is always speaking?" Do you believe that?

Since we are all unique, it makes sense we would each hear our Creator's voice differently. Some have audibly heard the voice of God, an actual voice heard with their physical ears. Others hear Him through specific and detailed dreams and visions. When I was dealing with breast cancer, God gave me detailed and specific dreams about what was coming. He knew I would need this preparation, an advanced warning. It was a blessing knowing He was involved in everything He allowed to touch my life. He knew cancer was going to be part of my story. He gave me advance notice because He knows how I operate. This is love.

I feel most alive and in touch with God when I am in nature. My senses come alive with the sounds, scents, and sensations. I have had my deepest times of communion in nature, whether in the forest, on a trail I'm hiking, sitting on the beach, or puttering in my backyard garden. It isn't an audible voice I hear, but it's what I sense. The brush of a playful breeze that cools my neck and ruffles my hair tells me that He cares and is present.

He speaks in the pounding surf and lapping waves, fear and wounding drawn out and away in the swell of the waves as I pour out my heart. Peace and awe fall over me amid the Redwoods; that glorious scent of pine, ancient growth, and strength remind me of His power and creativity. He has everything planned. It isn't safe and predictable, but it is good. Sitting under the stars and moon, I feel His majesty and Lordship cover me like protective wings. This feels safe; I am protected and fiercely guarded. My Father's eye is never off me. His eye is never off you.

Maybe you don't believe you have heard Him, but I believe you have. Keep an open heart and open ears. Ask Him how He wants to speak to you. I promise you He does. But He is a gentleman. He waits to be invited. Will you let Him in?

Perspective

COMPLAINTS. We all have them. Some are minor annoyances that come on strong but fade quickly, such as irritating drivers, long lines at the Starbucks drive-thru, internet annoyances, and teenage attitudes. Then there are those other complaints. The ones that stem from something deeper than mundane irritants, like unmet expectations, disappointments, loss, simmering anger, injustice, illness, and the list goes on. I have experienced all of these. Feelings of frustration, anger, and resentment that well up from these complaints can easily taint every interaction, experience, and relationship. Our filters get off-kilter and become skewed. This is a hard and debilitating way to live.

Recently, I came upon this jewel found in Habakkuk 2:1— "I will climb up into my watchtower now and wait to see what the Lord will say to me and how he will answer my complaint."

I visualize climbing up into a watchtower. As I ascend, things begin to change. I am no longer looking at the landscape the same way because my perspective changes the higher I climb. The complaint is still the same; the geography of the problems hasn't changed. However, the way I see them does.

In the watchtower, I am safe, secure, and protected. I have a 360-degree view of the terrain. I see how the landscape melds and molds together, how certain things must happen before other things can exist. If there is a mountain, there is an uphill climb that must take place before one can reach the pinnacle, just as there is a descent, sometimes into a valley or depression, that must be traversed before coming into a wide-open place; a space that is safer and easier to walk.

As I see more of the surrounding land, I realize it is quite beautiful, and how it all runs together in harmony. Rugged and dangerous mix with lovely, breathtaking, restful places; places that are safe and easy; places that are dangerous and even treacherous in spots. It all works together to be beautiful. Never minimizing or mocking the pain, hurt, and loss that life and situations bring, but focusing on a different perspective. Like a tapestry that takes shape and becomes lovely when all the threads are woven together just as they need to be, even if the process is long, tedious, and unclear.

God wants us to bring Him the hurt, rage, fear, and injustice. When we lay it before Him and go up into our watchtower to wait for His answer, He gives us His divine perspective. The problems are still there; it still hurts and frustrates and enrages, yet, when we get a glimpse of the full picture, when we look behind and see where we have come and remember all He's done, it gives all that lies ahead a new hue. A new filter through which to view our current complaints. He is with us. Always.

Climbing up into the watchtower is like a symbol of leaning into Jesus. There is safety in Him. As we lay the burdens before Him, that release allows Divine Perspective to come in and heal, mend and counsel; to comfort, love and change the view of the landscape to one of hope, healing, and transformation. This produces a whole new level of trust. Immense comfort and even joy can be found when I head up into the watchtower and wait. Peace is always there. Beauty will follow. When I see from a divine perspective, I know that nothing has been wasted. It was all necessary for what was to come. Alpha, Omega; beginning and the end.

How Do You Fit?

HAVE YOU EVER BEEN at church and experienced the uncomfortable feeling of not fitting in when it comes to how you encounter Jesus? Does it seem like the tried-and-true formula of experiencing Him doesn't work for you or that you never fully arrive; are somehow found lacking? You watch everyone nodding in earnest agreement when the sermon urges you to follow the formula of reading the Word daily, for a specific amount of time, in a certain place, in a specific position, saying specific things, and following a proven formula to bring you close to Jesus.

However, your Spirit is not connecting with this, and your attempts at following these rote formulas fall flat. Everyone is nodding and looking sagely about them, confirming that yes, this is how it must be done. The closeness you felt to Him as you worshipped just moments before seeps away, as doubt and failure cloud your thoughts. "Yes," says Satan, "you don't fit in the body of Christ; you can't even follow a simple formula to fill that void. Maybe you don't belong." Lies.

Hearing others say what we must do to be a strong Christian can be very crippling in our journey with Jesus. When you love Jesus, seek Him, and find Him, but are told it isn't enough, unless a formula is followed, it wounds and taints something that should be precious, intimate, and deep. A stench of doubt permeates the very thing Jesus celebrates about us, our uniquely individual personalities. No one is identical, better, more loved, more cherished, or more valuable. We each have a specific purpose, and that is beautiful.

I react, buck, and kick at being boxed into a formula for doing anything in life, especially when journeying with Jesus. I may not always outwardly thrash at the formulas, but in my mind and spirit, I do.

Spiritual disciplines are wonderful, necessary, and amazing things we get to use, as our personalities dictate. Some will pour over His word, intently study, and soak it in; others will worship and dance to connect with Him; some will pray without ceasing; and some share Jesus with strangers, while others sit silently in His presence, soaking Him up. Some of us need nature with our senses fully activated, experiencing Him through sights, sounds, and the wind in our faces. It's all good. So, go and connect with Him in the way He created you to. Be free and enjoy every second.

Morning at the Duck Pond

THE SUN hasn't been up for long, yet the pond is fully awake.

On a large moss-covered rock in one corner of the pond, the cormorant is sunning itself; fully spread wings welcome the warm sun.

Turtles occupy most of the warming rocks and gnarled old roots, jutting up from the still water; always watching, always aware; stout legs and webbed feet stretched out to soak in the warmth.

As I wander closer to the pond's edge, sleepy ducks regard me with curiosity, but they aren't afraid; others doze on, with heads tucked into cozy, feathery wings.

The proud Canadian geese continue nibbling grassy tidbits and bugs as I stroll by; a few venture a hiss or two, just to make sure we are on the same page.

The pond is still and quiet, yet it's not.

Human noises are blessedly absent, but morning greetings

and conversations are vivid and noisy; the rhythm of the pond is in full swing!

Cheerful, grounding, natural. Life lessons can be learned here; the Divine is all around.

Along the grassy edge of the pond, small fish and tadpoles congregate in the warm shallows as a ray of sun brings heat and light. Life.

My shadow causes a frantic, mass exodus as they dart in a mass of tiny tails and fins to safer waters. Ripples and bubbles mark their escape.

A large, silent turtle, with only the tip of its snout visible is waiting, slowly submerging in an effortless swim to its breakfast—the ebb and flow of life on the pond.

Along the edge of the pond, there is evidence of nests and bedded-down reeds, a few delicate eggshell pieces, and tufts of feathers and down. Home for a family of ducks; their safe place, warm and tucked away.

The insistent chirping of a red-winged blackbird signals that I am too close for comfort to his family home in the tall, fully-leafed tree in front of me.

I move gingerly around this part of the pond as he begins to dive and swoop at me, clearly indicating that I'm a visitor here. Respect.

Rounding one side of the pond, a mama and her ducklings dart and swim through the smooth glass water, nibbling up tidbits as they happily cluck and chatter. She steers them toward the middle of the pond. Cautious. The ripples they leave behind swirl and eddy, then disappear as the still water swallows them up. Calm restored.

Random splishes and splashes can be heard as turtles slip into the water like small submarines; tiny, pointy heads can be seen as they break the surface to keep a sharp eye on the pond bank; scouts that watch and wait.

The green heron, the master fisherman, is tucked up and underneath the mass of reeds on a thin root poking up through the water. He patiently waits in stillness and silence. He knows food is just below the surface and silently waits for his opportunity. Patience.

Rippled movement catches my eye. I carefully make my way to the edge of the pond, curiosity brimming. Is it the river otter back again to fish and dine on crawdads and little fish?

No, it is a large, orangey, iridescent fish. Its tail poking up and rippling the water like a miniature shark's fin as it roots in the murky, muddy water under the gnarled old tree with the beautiful leafy branches.

I am captivated.

I sink to my feet, watching it go about its business, gracefully moving and swishing as it searches for a treasure hidden in the murky pond. Trust.

A sudden cacophony of honking and quacking breaks apart the loudly peaceful pond, as a goose announces its displeasure; wings and webbed feet flapping and dashing into the pond, causing a few moments of panic and unrest as others follow suit.

Quickly, all is calm, and everyone goes about their business as if nothing has happened. Ritual, rhythm, and order restored. Life at the pond.

The bench tucked in under the beautiful tree, with weepy branches skimming the water, beckons to me.

Resting here in the shade, I try to blend in quietly, allowing nature to return to its busy activities and the turtles to relax their ever vigilant and rigid watch. There is always one who stalks, silently tracking my movements.

As my eyes roam, I notice that the trees and flowering plants are always reaching up to the sky, their source of life; branches and tender shoots going up, up.

Even in the seasons of autumn and winter, when skies are grey, and the sun seems scarce, their branches always seek light and reach upward. They know Who sustains them.

Some of these trees are gnarled and funky with twists and crimps, bends and burned out, broken up places, yet up; they always point up.

The simplicity of creation looks to the Creator to protect, provide, and sustain as the seasons and cycles of life move ever onward.

My life resembles these tenacious trees, with their broken branches, crooked spots, and seasons of beauty and abundance, fully leafed and lovely.

Seasons come and go, ebb and flow as the divine tapestry of our lives are woven by a Master weaver; intersecting pain and beauty; abundance and lack. Always with arms and face lifted to the Source of Life.

Permission to Rest

MARK 6:31—"Then, because so many people were coming and going that they did not even have a chance to eat, he said to them, "'Come with me by yourselves to a quiet place and get some rest.'"

Jesus and His disciples had little if any leisure time during His time of ministry. The crowds were relentless. People were anxious to be near Jesus, to listen to His revolutionary teaching that set them free and released them from bondage, fear, and legalism. They heard He had the power to heal them physically and spiritually, so they came in droves with their illness and pain, with those suffering from demonic harassment and chains, for a chance to see Him, touch Him, be healed.

Being fully God and fully man, Jesus felt the physical and mental exhaustion of always being "on" and the deep fatigue of being surrounded by the hurting, needy, and lost. So, Jesus rested. He was diligent in removing Himself and His disciples for periods of refreshment, and spiritual and physical re-filling, so they could return encouraged and strengthened for the next task. He gave Himself and His disciples permission to rest, eat, and get away from the urgency of humanity knocking at the door of their hearts.

Our days may not be filled with healing the sick and enemy-harassed, or with traveling dusty roads that parch the mouth, or teaching on hillsides in the hot sun, but He knows what our days are filled with—chaotic relationships, disappointments, dreams that seem far from being realized, illnesses, past regrets that haunt our peace and the daily annoyances and offenses that threaten to become bigger than they need to be.

Jesus understands the physical and mental exhaustion of taking care of everyone else and the things we take on that are not ours to carry. Is He calling you to go with Him for a spell, to refresh and soothe your mind, spirit, and body? He is giving you permission to rest. So, rest.

Faces of Peace

Peace has many different faces and invades every situation. It can be quiet and unobserved, waiting to be noticed. It happens in the wee hours of the morning while rocking a tired, cranky baby, praying for rest and calm until suddenly you feel it—peace. It was there waiting, gently and softly. Rest. Peace. All is well; you are safe and secure. Sheltered.

Peace is there on an ordinary day when things are flowing smoothly, life is pleasant, and people are kind.

Peace is there in the absence of storms, just as real, alive, and powerful as it is during grueling trials that seem endless. Peace is there when the Doctor takes a deep breath and says, "I'm so sorry. You have breast cancer." Peace keeps you from losing yourself to terror when desperation blasts in and you feel like you are drowning and have no control. Peace is there in the middle of the "what-ifs," saying, "Yes! What if you are healed? What if you are well taken care of and never alone in this? What if you are held in arms that are bigger than all your fears, sheltered amid all this hurt and chaos? What if? What if…"

Peace reminds you that it was there before this storm hit, and it will be there forever after. Peace lifts your face and asks you to fasten your gaze steadily into the eyes of Jesus, the Prince of Peace. It is Jesus; peace is Jesus. Such calm, such safety, such rest.

My searching and desire for peace lead directly to Jesus. I won't find it inside myself. That will fall short every time. I have tried being self-reliant and strong enough. The One who created me, when I was but a thought in His mind, wants me to feel peace, to know He is working out all things for good, according to that beautiful, unique plan that is my life. Your life. The time He took to carefully place us right where we are, surrounded by the people and circumstances that He brought into being, shows that He knows what He is doing. We win because He is victorious over death and sin. It is ok to not know what to do if you know the One who does. It is ok not to have it figured out. He already did that.

Can we walk out not knowing? We do it every day, don't we? We wake up and go. However, the going is easier when we understand that He has us in His hands and that nothing comes toward us that He has not first filtered through hands of love, a mind of infinite wisdom, and a heart that loves us fiercely, intensely, and intimately. This is a wild love. It is not tame or controllable. Yet, in this fierce and protective love, we find the greatest of peace. Jesus.

Truth

GOD LOVES YOU. He created you and knows everything about you. Your weaknesses and struggles are not driving Him away from you. He is there always, as close as your next breath. Go ahead, inhale. You are seen and known; you have God's undivided attention. You are here for a reason; you are not a mistake or a random happening. There is a path carefully laid out for you. It is for you and no one else. The heart of the Father knew exactly what He was doing when you were created to walk that path and make a difference to those in your sphere. Do you know that there are conversations happening in heaven about you? You are always on His mind, engraved on His hands and His heart.

Those places in your heart that hurt, the place in your soul that has been so wounded, have not gone unnoticed by God. He saw, He knows, and He grieves. If you give it to Him, He will take it and redeem it; He wants to do that for you. Don't you know that is why He came? He will restore and transform those places that seem too lost, too broken, too ugly. Those places will become places of beauty in His hands. The secret hurt isn't hidden from Him. He knows all about anger and hatred, injustice, bitterness, resentments, failures and victories, and joyful A-ha moments.

He looks on you with eyes of love and compassion, joy, and mercy. You are His child. Talk to Him. He loves to hear our voices, like melodies and harmonies in His ears. To our ears, the song may sound dreadfully out of tune, but the sound of your voice, my voice, is like incense to Him. It is a thing of beauty when we speak to Him, and He responds, deep calls to deep; Spirit speaking to spirit. It is a holy communion. When we do not have words to speak, His Spirit is there, and He knows. No big words, wild gestures, or loud voices are needed with Him. He is there in the silence when there are no words. Speaking His name is enough.

Day at the Beach

THE EARLY MORNING SUN offers the promise of warmth and expectation.

An indolent day at the beach is exactly what is needed!

Arms laden with a beach bag full of vittles, sunscreen, and a towel, I discover the perfect spot to settle in for the day.

Cliffs behind me, ocean before me, sun above me, sand below.

Perfection. Shelter. Peace.

My little space is set up; all is in order and ready for me to be one with the breeze and old-Earth smell of brine and life and decay.

Shoes off, sunscreen on, now to the water.

Contradictions.

That is what I see in the ocean, yet also safety, born out of the ancient rhythms of the Earth—forever marching on, steady and unyielding.

The tide's constancy is relentless, untamable, fierce; all without apology, the ocean does what it is meant to do.

The water laps and rushes and chases my feet, startling and elemental in its coldness. Invigorating and inspiring.

The birds, crabs, and tiny sea creatures count on the unchanging ways of the ocean because it is life to them. The ocean gives, and these creatures take.

But I think the ocean is also a taker. It takes the worries, stress, fears, and uncertainties in life; it takes words spoken and wept and screamed by those who walk the beach looking for answers, solace, and peace. We push those things out of our hearts, and the ocean pulls them into itself.

A lovely dance.

Perhaps this is what God does for us. He takes all the fear, rage, worry, and tears that we spew out into Himself and pulls them away from us as we release it all to Him. He is fierce, constant, untamable, mysterious, and present. He gives life; He is love; we rely on Him.

Back at my sanctuary, the sand under my legs and back is so warm, relaxing, and inviting. It is solid and permanent; warmth leeches into my chilled bones, lulled to a drowsy peacefulness.

With closed eyes and warm sun baking down in pleasant coziness, I notice my other senses stirred; susurrating waves whisper and breathe, birds call overhead; somewhere, a dog is barking.

That scent of salt floats on the ever-present breeze along with notes of a barbecue and the cloying scent of flowers.

Drowsy and dreamy, my mind wanders in that half-dreaming state of blissful rest.

The sun has shifted in the sky, and there is a slight chill in the air. How long have I been lying here?

Hunger gnaws, so here come the snacks.

Seagulls make an appearance and scold and demand that I share, watching closely every move I make. I share.

Before packing up, it's time for a walk.

There are footprints going before me in the sea-soaked sand, and I wonder whose they are and what secrets they've spoken to the sea today.

Interesting how before long, all traces of my footprints will be washed away, as if I had never walked here; as if the past is washed away and cleaned up and brand-new sand is offered up for a new direction, new footprints, new promises.

Jesus cleans up our lives like this; the old washed away, the new offered up; clean, lovely, and ready for a new journey.

Sun dipping down, air quite cool, water coming higher; my signal to call it a day.

Heading to the car, I feel rested, new, and cleansed, a little wild and wooly from the rawness of the ocean and its wild and chaotic yet perfectly ordered dance.

Seashells

WHEN I WAS at the beach not long ago, I sat on the sand, soaking up the sun. This beach was full of beautiful treasures washed up by the waves. I noticed some interesting-looking shells lying near my resting spot, so I gave them a closer look. Some were very intricate in shape and color, while others were smooth with a few rough edges. Some were simple and sleek with muted colors, while others were brighter and more vibrant, with fascinating nooks and crannies. I piled them in front of me on the sand and imagined how each one became what it was, what its journey through the ocean might have been like, and how far it traveled before spitting up on the sand for beach lovers to gasp over and bring home as lovely treasures.

Observing the force of the waves breaking on the shore, these shells went through a lot to get where they ended up, some whole and intact, others broken and a bit beat up, but pretty and interesting all the same. These shells were uprooted from where they were comfortable and established on the ocean floor. The incessant pull of the tide and other sea creatures disrupting them, forced the creatures inside the shells to move, hide, or break just to survive.

Depending on the distance traveled, the severity of the storms weathered, and the amount of time the shells were thrown into the rocks and ocean floor had a huge impact on how they arrived on the beach and what condition they were in when their journey ended. Isn't this like us? When we come to Jesus and allow Him to be the center of our lives, don't we feel a bit worse for wear? For some of us, the journey was not as arduous as it was for others, so we arrived like clean, shiny shells with just a few rough edges. For others, the journey was long and difficult, and we arrived broken and battered. Still, others arrived with a vibrancy that captures the attention, with fascinating nooks and crannies.

The wonderful thing about these shells is that each one is beautiful in its own way. Each one speaks to someone different. Each one of us, with our intricacies, brokenness, vibrancy, funky nooks and crannies, or smooth edges, is needed to make this world complete, to speak to other people right where they are in life. Walking on a beach and seeing only identical shells would be boring and devoid of life and mystery. I imagine Jesus looking at each of us, gasping in delight and snatching us up as His precious treasures.

Soul Garden

IN THE EARLY LIGHT of this spring morning, I survey my garden. Hot coffee warms my chilled hands. Birds line up along the edge of the fence and sit in the leafy, budding plum tree. The squirrels peer and chatter from the branches of the fig and apple trees, letting me know I'm late. They wait for the thistle, peanuts, and cracked corn they expect me to toss out for them.

From my seat at the patio table, I see that the new plants I have carefully placed in the earth, along with the returning perennials, are thriving and sending up their tender shoots. The time, energy, sweat, and joy that fertilized them are paying off. It is exciting to see new life and growth return after a season of quiet resting.

Mother Nature begins her whispering and coaxing, and the tender new growth responds. So much happens below the surface before these tender stems and leaves are ready to push upward and outward. Root systems are established and require a certain amount of strength and depth before sending up the shoots. It's all carefully orchestrated and set in motion when the Creator determines the timing is just right.

As I admire my garden, a thought begins to take shape in my mind, and I wonder where Jesus is going with it. What if the fellow humans I encounter in life are like a garden of the soul? I start with a plot of earth and carefully turn, work, and fertilize the dirt with time, tears, laughter, and love. As I bump up against these people, I smile in delight as I find just the ones to add to my soul garden. They fit perfectly! I scoop them up, carefully and gently planting them, nurturing and tending, removing weeds and obstacles, giving time and attention. I watch as tendrils of common interest, branches of stability and longevity, flowers of laughter, buds of adventure, and the fragrance of kindness and vulnerability perfume my garden. Everything blends well, and the beauty is nourishing to my soul. Peaceful. Safe. I belong.

However, not all the flowers and bushes are thriving and healthy in my soul garden. Some are old, spent, and have lived out their flowering season, taking up the space where another might thrive. The annuals were there for a season and won't return but leave behind nice memories. Some have become hardened, woody, and impenetrable, no longer blooming or showing any growth. Others stubbornly resist any sort of pruning, fertilizing or change and stay stumped and thwarted, no longer lovely. The Master Gardener says it is time to begin weeding.

Weeding the soul garden can be sad, hard, and frightening but necessary. I get to choose, and so do you, who and what is allowed to take up space there. These choices can mean life, joy, and flourishing for our souls or stunted growth, disappointment, and hurt. A lot is bound up in the roots of who I allow in that sacred place. Layer upon layer of energy, laughter, tears, shared history, and effort are mixed and blended to keep it all alive. The dying back, pruning, and even the uprooting of those that were carefully planted can be brutal and harsh, leaving a hole and a void for loneliness to sprout up.

I believe that Jesus views that hole and the loneliness as a prime plot of land in which to plant Himself. It is impossible to have a need that He cannot meet. In the loneliness of the weeding season, He will pour into us all of Himself. He is enough. We are seen, we are safe, and we are known. Our needs will be met, and our roots will be strengthened and built up for the growing season that is to come. The dirt in our soul garden will be nurtured and watered with His wisdom, healing, and joy, but He will sift, filter, and discard all that is not in sync with His master plan.

That is painful, yet we know there is beauty in this pain. He knows why a once vibrant and healthy-looking part of our soul garden now needs to be pruned or uprooted and completely removed. He sees all that is going on underneath the surface, where growth takes place and roots either thrive or rot. He knows when our souls need a respite from nurturing others, so we can be nurtured, replenished, and tended to with love, attention, and mercy by the Master Gardener.

The world and all that is in it is still at His beck and call. He is fully aware of those others who are coming along in the next seasons, those who will once again cause us to gasp, smile, and make room in our garden for a bloom with the exact fragrance needed, in just the right season, for our souls to thrive. There is peace in knowing that after an anonymous winter of quiet cultivation by our Father, a lovely, bursting spring is waiting to captivate us with the joy of new growth and unexpected blooms. Psalm 126:5-6 says, "Those who plant in tears will harvest with shouts of joy. They weep as they go to plant their seed, but they sing as they return with the harvest."

Angels

I BELIEVE we encounter angels and their divine presence as they carry out their God-ordained work among us, more often than we realize. We can miss these carefully orchestrated meetings if we are not actively looking for God's presence and movement in our lives. The awe-inspiring encounters that we witness are often minimized to chance, circumstances, planets aligning, and serendipity. We are a busy, self-reliant, proud species, we humans. Admitting that Someone greater than ourselves keeps a close and constant watch over our every move, breath, and encounter, is hard to swallow when pride slithers in and whispers that we don't need anyone or anything. We've got this all under control. The idea that God already knows and has breathed into existence everything we will experience in every moment of our lives is almost too much to bear. It is much easier to be fanciful and think that we have done, seen, figured it all out.

Psalm 91:11-12—"For He will order His angels to protect you wherever you go. They will hold you up with their hands, so you won't even hurt your foot on a stone."

What might an angel encounter be like? It won't always be phenomenal, historical, widely broadcast, and visible to multitudes of witnesses. It won't always be a cast of heavenly hosts singing and welcoming the Savior into the world. But it is still divine, miraculous, and history-making for the one visited by an angel.

Maybe it looks like an accident that should have happened, yet miraculously did not. It could be a rendezvous with a stranger so timely and perfect that there isn't another option except for an angel encounter. Perhaps someone shows up at exactly the right time, provides aid and kindness, and completely disappears before a word of thanks can be offered; no one else saw or came across that person but you, and it's truly beyond explanation, but it isn't, is it? God commands His angels to be all around and about us every place we go. No, they are not God and are not to be worshipped, but they are commanded by God. They are about His business in our lives. This brings me comfort, even though bad things still happen. Not every sad and tragic thing is kept from us, which is beyond what I can explain. But God knows, and He sees, and He is filtering everything that touches us.

Several years ago, my son and I were on a road trip. All was fine and low-key until it wasn't. A car passing us suddenly lost the entire driver's side wheel. It shot straight in front of our car, bounced, and flew backward, heading directly for our windshield. We were in the fast lane with a guardrail to the right and the swerving car with the missing wheel to the left. In slow motion, I watched in terror as that wheel shot straight at us. At the absolute last moment, it veered completely opposite its trajectory path, physically impossible, as if something with an incredible amount of force pushed it, and the wheel hit the guard rail and stopped. My son and I would have been killed or gravely injured that day had angels not intervened and brought that spinning tire under God's control. The divine among us.

There was a time a casual walk in the park became a frightening confrontation with a stranger intent on harming me. The man and the danger were circumvented and not permitted, as I felt Jesus telling me exactly what to do and say, and I physically felt His command and His angels' presence blocking the event meant for evil. Luke 4:10 says, "For it is written: He will command his angels concerning you to guard you carefully."

I believe angel encounters are happening all the time, in the mundane and trivial, the frightening and funny, the lovely and tragic, the victory and joy. Hebrews 13:2 says, "Do not forget to show hospitality to strangers, for by so doing, some people have shown hospitality to angels without knowing it." Eyes open, hearts receptive, ears listening. The divine is all around you.

The Ancient Paths

JEREMIAH 6:16 says, "This is what the Lord says: Stand at the crossroads and look; ask for the ancient paths, ask where the good way is, and walk in it, and you will find rest for your souls. But you said, 'We will not walk in it.'"

I picture a traveler setting out alone on a pilgrimage to find "the good way." Someone who feels restless, dissatisfied, and unfulfilled in the world and their place in it, searching for meaning and significance. I imagine this traveler is tired, dusty, and thirsty, longing for a place to rest. The journey has been a long one—a lifetime.

Up ahead, our traveler spies a crossroads where different paths intersect and head off in completely different directions. There is an oasis at the crossroads, some sheltering trees where our sojourner can stop and think about which path to take. Where does each one lead? What if our traveler chooses the wrong way? Will the journey continue without leading to what they want most, which is peace and safety for a banged-up soul that is wounded and weary, longing for healing, simplicity, and to just belong?

I imagine our weary traveler surveying each path, looking at the options, and wondering what to do. One path looks wider and more comfortable, the other narrow and rocky. What to do? Hidden in the shadows of a small grove of trees, our traveler spots a man reclining in the cool shade. Feeling relief that there is someone here who may know the answer, the traveler heads over and asks, "Which is the good way?"

The man looks at the weary soul in front of him and asks, "What is it that you want? These paths lead in very different directions, my friend, so choose wisely. One, the good way, will lead you on a narrower path, with areas that are not easy to navigate with obstacles you will have to go around, over, or through. There will be mountains and valleys. The going will not always be easy, but the end will bring you more joy and life than you could imagine. There will be beauty along this path, but pain, too. You will find rest for your weary soul, but you must follow the One who leads you and not stray off on your own. Many have followed this path before you; their footsteps can be seen and followed along the way."

The traveler likes the idea of beauty and rest, but pain and obstacles, giving up control? "What about the other path?" he asks, "Tell me about it."

The man sighs and begins speaking, "The other path, well, it will seem easier, smoother, wider. It will appear to be well-traveled and allow you to chart the course. There are many crossroads you will have to navigate on this path, and you will be doing it on your own. You will choose which way to go, and you will reap the consequences. The footsteps of those who went before you will be smudged, obscure, and not easy to see. Those other travelers will not offer you wisdom; they will be concentrating on themselves and making their own way."

The traveler has a lot to think about. Having a guide to navigate those rough places sounds inviting. Peace and rest are promised at the end of this path. There will be beauty but also pain. Beauty in the pain? The other path sounds nice. Easy, smooth, wide. Obstacles, yes, but the ability to decide how to navigate them and being able to say that you arrived because of your own wisdom. But the man didn't say that at the end of this path, there would be rest and healing. He didn't say what would be found at the end.

So, what do you choose, fellow traveler? When you come to the crossroads, which path will you choose? The one with the promise of rest for your weary soul? Does the pull of being in control and having a wider, easier path call out to you? Will you take the path that is well worn with the sandals of men and women who chose Jesus, the ancient paths with footprints of the One who knows how to navigate? Or will you see that path laid before you and say, "No, I will not walk in it?"

Come Away

I'M UP EARLY. A restless, unsettled day led to a similar night of sleep.

Rest is elusive, thoughts scattered.

Warm, earthy, steamy coffee warms my hands; my eyes glaze over, mind swirling.

Through the open kitchen window, the morning air carries the faint scent of jasmine and cool earth.

The house is warm, but the fragrant air is inviting and full of promise. It beckons.

A friendly breeze, a puff of soft air, calls to me from the musical notes of the wind chimes, "Come out." I go out.

My favorite bench is canopied by the looming butterfly bush; its purple, fragrant blooms toss and wave, encouraging me to come.

I do.

The cold marble of my bench, as I sit, is in stark contrast to the warmth of my hands around the child-painted coffee cup I carry with me. I love Mommy, it proudly shouts from its brightly painted surface. That brings a smile.

Also, some tears.

I don't feel so loveable of late. Irritable. Tired. Frustrated. Not loveable. Chaotic, possibly.

Looking at the flowers in the planter tubs next to my bench, I see chaos, at first.

Looking closer, I notice that the random way I planted these lovelies is quite beautiful. Patterns emerge amidst the seemingly random design.

There is order here in the planter, despite the chaos, and it is so lovely! Yes! Yes, it is.

Must goodness, beauty, and happiness be meticulously ordered, spaced, and arranged to be acceptable? Must I understand it? This revelation makes me smile, breathe deeply, and inhale life.

The rising sun glitters at me on the feathery water of the stone birdbath. Winking and spunky, I want to laugh with it at the possibilities of the new day.

I feel my back and shoulders relax; everything isn't wiry and tense, ready for flight. Calm. Peace. Is that joy?

The breeze caresses the back of my neck with cool, kind fingers, barely a whisper against my ear.

What was that? I close my eyes, try to still my mind, and just be.

I hear it now. You are speaking, but no words are spoken.

The peaceful scent of jasmine and butterfly bush blooms tell me all is well.

The stable, steady, ancient scent of dirt reminds me that new life is all around; rebirth is waiting daily for me to acknowledge it.

The breeze whispers that I'm never alone. You will never leave me. I remember; I know.

I see in the riotous, chaotic colors and placement of the flowers that You have patterned and woven my life together in a tapestry that appears to be a random intersection of lines and curves, and hills and dales; yet is something far more beautiful, ordered, and perfected than I can imagine.

You see the entire picture of me, and You call it lovely; You call me lovely. I am enough because of You.

You have dried my tears and captured them in a bottle that holds all of them. In place of frustration, acceptance has taken root. Not a resigned, sighing acceptance, but an acceptance of the unique journey I am on with all the ups and downs I know will come.

My place in Your arms as chosen, loved, and redeemed is reconfirmed on my little marble bench. I am enough. I just needed to come away with You for a spell. You remind me I'm Yours, and all will be well.

Heart Words

PSALM 27:8 says, "My heart has heard You say, 'Come and talk with me.' And my heart responds, 'Lord, I am coming.'"

Challenges. Distractions. Life. Choices to make, priorities to set, goals to reach. Maybe no calamity befalls me or mine, nothing life or death happens on a particular day, but sometimes it does. Some days I feel hollow, disappointed, irritable, short-changed, overlooked, and misunderstood. I spend time pondering these hollow, worn-out feelings, wondering where they are coming from and how to get rid of them.

So, I endeavor to "set aside" time for Jesus. I will read my Bible these many minutes, read X number of chapters, pray for this amount of time, and all will be well. I will start with thanksgiving, then confession, and praying for all the needs of others. Next, I will pray for God to orchestrate my time and talent and use it for His good and glory. That is the formula, right? There is nothing wrong with focused Bible study and structured time with God. Isn't that what everyone says is the way to do it? So why is the formula not working? Why is the simmering, brewing frustration still there? Why is the discontent and irritation still bubbling and buffeting my heart and spirit? It is a vague, foggy sense of something being off, like a minuscule rock stuck in your sock that you can't quite find but is so bothersome that it becomes the only thing you focus on but never quite find.

With French Roast and some creamy foam in my favorite I LOVE MOM mug, I found my spot at the patio table, with my Bible and all the necessary accompaniments at hand...and sat there. Nothing. As I sat, I noticed birds darting all over my yard, content going about their business, exactly as God designed them. They sang. They squabbled. They moved on. They came back at a better time to grab an open spot on the feeder. They didn't sit and feel sad that they didn't get the ideal spot on the feeder. They were creative in how they forced themselves into a space that, at first glance, didn't look possible.

This reminded me of Matthew 6:25, which says, "Therefore I tell you, do not be anxious about your life, what you will eat or what you will drink, nor about your body, what you will put on. Is not life more than food and the body more than clothing? Look at the birds of the air: they neither sow nor reap nor gather into barns, and yet your heavenly Father feeds them. Are you not of more value than they? But seek first the kingdom of God and his righteousness, and all these things will be added to you."

Seek first the kingdom of God. Seek. How do I do that?

My careful formula isn't easing those feelings and filling those voids. And the formula isn't always genuine. Ahhhh, there it is. Genuine. Raw. Unscripted. These words are the exact opposite of formula yet pierced my heart. I long for these words to be real in my relationship with Jesus. As the light breeze flipped the pages of my open Bible, Psalm 27 shows up. Specifically, Psalm 27:8, "My heart has heard You say, 'Come and talk with me.' And my heart responds, 'Lord, I am coming.'" He is asking me to come and talk to Him, and my heart is leaping at the chance to do that! Nothing scripted, plotted, or planned. There is not a wrong way to come before Him. He said, "Come and talk with me." That speaks of intimacy, closeness, trust, and desire to be fully known.

This is what I really want; to be known in all the goodness, confusion, humor, failures, and victories. Wouldn't it be lovely to just be and not need a constant dialogue pouring from your mouth? When my son was younger, he told me I use too many words, and it exhausts him. It was funny, but wow, that is truth right there! Too many words. How lovely, peaceful, and restoring to be in the presence of my Father and not have to say words! Isn't that what the heart is all about? No words, big solutions, and hour-long flowery prayers, but presence, depth, and intimacy that doesn't always need an audible voice. Deep calling to deep, deep restoring and transforming deep.

I am finding my answers as I write this out. Yes, life is going to happen, and I can't do a thing about it. The balm needed to soothe and let go of those hollow, disappointed, irritable, short-changed, overlooked, and misunderstood feelings will not be found in a rote formula. No. My Father showed me His formula this morning on the patio in my everyday life, with my dogs nosing around the flower beds and birds scolding and singing. He asked my heart to come and hang out with Him. So I will, and I won't say a word.

He Will See To It

I'M TIRED, weary; some days weary to the literal bone. My heart and soul have questions that I know I will not get answers to on this side of heaven. That is not what overthinkers want to hear! My mind strives and spins in search of the "whys," the "should haves," and the "if onlys."

Worry and overthinking are beliefs that God will not get this right, whatever the "this" is for us. It is belief gone wrong. I must go back to what I know about the Lord. I must purposefully shift my mind to remember His promises and character. It's hard and deliberate, and I don't always want to make an effort. I'm worn out and angry. I must look below the surface of all that is swirling and clamoring, the noise and chaos trying to lay claim to my peace and faith. I need to remember all the ways I have been healed and provided for, all the ways He has taken those things I saw as evil and impossible and used them for good; miracles that only I have seen but profoundly changed me.

In times of loneliness, He has been near and spoken beautiful, soul-deep words and promises that no human could provide but Him, words that would have been drowned out by expectations of others and their views and opinions. It is remembering that not a single thing happens that He does not allow to first pass through His hands before it can touch me, touch you. This remembering does not make the pain, loneliness, and fear go away. We are still humans with emotions and breaking points. But the Lord sees, and He will see to it. The Lord always sees what they did and didn't do, how you were treated, what the Dr does and doesn't say. The life-tapestry woven for us is beyond our limited vision but is always seen and handcrafted by a unique God-design that is never wrong, too much, too little, or inadequate. It is just what is needed. It's exactly enough.

Can we pause for a minute and listen soul-deep? Ah, the mysterious, lovely, and precious things He wants us to know! Below the surface, there is good and beauty, and it has happened; it is happening and intertwining amid reality, and God sees it all. He sees the tired body, the wounded heart, the panic and striving, as well as the victories, joy, and laughter. He sees what is coming in the next minute, the next month, the next year. He will see to it.

Here is the beauty of faith; we may not see the provision right away, and at times, it won't feel like provision and tender care at all, but that honestly doesn't matter, does it? If we have faith, even if that faith is a tiny, dirtied thread tossed, frayed, and tangled by life, we can trust we are well looked after and well-loved. Hope. It is not easy, but possible because rest is found here. Blessed, beloved, beautiful rest and He will see to it.

...in nature

The Cabin

SPRING

A BRIGHT morning with clean, clear air; the smell of new growth is rejuvenating.

Light and promising, the still early sharpness of new spring dances on the light breeze.

A cup of English Breakfast tea with bacon on toast sits with me on the high deck overlooking the meadow that soon blends into the forest.

I smile and greet the flowers dotting the meadow below me with their heavy, waving heads, their pale colors teasing at the intensity to come.

Welcome Spring!

Green-yellow shoots of new grass force their way up through the gentle earth, stretching and coming alive under the light-yellow sun.

The morning is already noisy, full of life, energetic.

The happy creek is splashing and rushing in full force; water from melted snow forcing its way down the mountain; tender reeds and cattails making a brave show of guarding the greening banks.

Birds have been up since dawn, delighting in the awakening bugs, fallen seeds, and promises of good things to come.

It is time to hike; time to get out there and discover the hidden gems, which are just awakening and coming to life after a long winter of silent sleep.

The ground is still soft and springy, pliant under my slightly muddy boots.

Brisk walking, blood is pumping; alert for woodland creatures also enjoying the new birth and tender delicacies all around.

The shining lake seems happy, full to the brim with birds and creatures and bugs galore, busily gorging on spring's buffet; the light breeze ruffling the water lifts the soul.

Pleasant afternoon turns to cool evening; sun going down.

Sunset on the deck during the evening meal of pasta and salad with lemony iced tea. Lovely.

Forest quieting; night falling.

SUMMER

Rising early to savor the cool of the morning, the sun is peeking over the treetops.

Ginger Peach tea with granola, fresh fruit, and yogurt accompany me to the deck.

Hello Summer!

It's a lazy morning; creatures are up and stirring, but the pace is less frenetic.

The babble of the creek has taken on a more languid pace, and I can just make out some footprints along its bank. Raccoon? Skunk?

Birds call and swoop, coaxing young ones to take flight; bugs and other delicacies brought to the wide, young mouths waiting inside downy nests.

Meadow flowers and grasses are tall now, twisting and dipping in the warming, lazy breeze.

The pace is certainly slower.

It's time to layer up for the hike. Pleasant now, but the afternoon promises to be warm and close.

Canteens of water, beach towel, swimsuit. To the lake!

Cool mountain water zings the skin and wakes up the senses after that first daring plunge!

Warm, drowsy, pine-scented air creates the perfect backdrop for napping on the old beach towel.

Memories of camping and outdoor adventures flit through my mind as I gently doze.

Sleepy and comfy.

Watching and listening to scurrying, rustling sounds in the reeds by the lake; family of ducks skimming the lake for water bugs, tiny frogs, and dangling berry bushes.

Duck family leaves behind ripples that spiral outward toward the shore.

Heading back to fire up the grill, lovely night to barbecue, and drink chilled white wine as the sun goes down, leaving a fiery trail on the horizon.

Sun has set; here come the marshmallows, grahams, and chocolate bars.

The evening is still and pleasant, perfect for s'mores and stories.

Forest quieting; night falling.

AUTUMN

A chill in the morning air; sleepy sun pushes over the horizon; animals stirring.

Hot coffee with cream, warm oatmeal with brown sugar, golden butter, and walnuts heads out to the deck with me.

Cheers, Autumn!

The chair is cool to the touch. Warm hoodie and yoga pants are just right for this crisp morning.

Warm but less intense sunlight filters down through the beginning to be bare branches, leaving a warm impression. Lovely.

The air has that certain and distinctive fall scent of browning leaves, dusty earth, and crisp air that isn't quite ready to mellow into deep winter—the comforting scent of pine.

The creek water pushes on, but with a slower gurgle, a gentle flow. Animal tracks at the edges; areas that are flattened down from what remains of a creature bed.

There are resilient, strong, stubborn grasses and flowers that are not yet ready to relax; they persist and bring color to a waning meadow and forest.

Time to hike. Hiking in autumn demands layers.

The warmer meadow where the sun still reaches and pours warmth onto backs and shoulders; then deeper into the woods with that unmistakable chill of the forest; fresh and chill, it demands a bit faster pace to keep comfortable.

That lovely, primal scent of pine.

Boots kick up a bit of dust, that leftover pliant earth from spring.

The lake is restful, the last vestiges of birds calling and making their Southward plans.

A bit too chilly for a dip in the calm water.

A calm and peaceful place to sit among fallen leaves and turning grasses and read until the autumn sun begins its descent.

Chipmunks and fluffy grey squirrels are chattering, roaming the branches and fallen leaves for those precious seeds and nuts that will be hidden away.

Scurrying and intent on seeking and finding provision.

Winter is coming.

The lit grill gives off welcome warmth as aromas of grilling vegetables, and juicy steaks fill the air around the cozy cabin. Potatoes are baking in the oven.

Red wine with dinner on the deck; sunlight fading; s'mores make their last appearance of the season.

A warm fire might be nice tonight.

Forest quieting; night falling.

WINTER

Blankets feel so warm in the cold morning; is it time to get up?

All is quiet outside the cabin. The watery sun seems to be struggling, too.

Rise and grab long, warm, heavy sweatpants and sweatshirt plus thick fuzzy socks.

First, hot coffee with cream; the mug sends warmth to already chilled hands.

Stoking up the fire again, warmth begins to infuse the chilly cabin.

Ah, Winter! You've arrived!

The second cup of steaming coffee accompanies me to the deck.

I must smell the freezing, chill air; so brisk it takes the breath away.

There it is! That crisp and lovely scent of pine. Refreshing!

Nowhere to sit with the coffee since the chairs are covered in ice.

Brave birds cover the bird feeder and relish the seeds I've put there for them; fluffed feathers make them look like plump, roly-poly little things.

More coffee, eggs, sausage, and toast go with me to the little table by the window as I watch the winter morning unfold.

Fire crackling well now; it should last for a bit.

Donning a hat, gloves, scarf, heavy jacket, boots; out I go to brave the cold and see the meadow and forest that winter has created.

No one is really out and about this morning.

Evidence of creature activity is all around, but those brave souls must already be back in warm, earthy dens, watching me from hollowed-out logs or nests in tree branches, wondering at the sight of me.

Trudging on for a bit; breathing in the wintry, piney air; chilled nose, ears, and chin; time to turn back.

The idea of a warm blanket, hot water with lemon, comfy slipper socks by the fire with my book is too strong of a call.

Shedding layers and climbing under the blanket, I relax and am swept away by the book.

Clouds have rolled in while I read. Brisk wind crept up and is rattling bare branches. Colder.

Dinner tonight will be hot bubbling soup and warm bread that I took a break from reading to prepare.

Back under the blanket, watching the fire, I hear the shushing sound of ticking snow on the deck.

Tomorrow morning will be white.

The forest is quiet; night has fallen on the cabin.

Meandering

HIGH in the forested mountain, a burst of water comes bubbling up. Why it started there in that hidden place is a mystery. Spreading out, it searches for the path it is to follow. There isn't one readily visible, so with tenacity and confidence, it presses forward, looking for that indentation, the hollowed decline in the ground. Success!

Following the downward dip in the ground, the water flows. Sometimes it seems to follow an exact, obvious path that makes perfect sense, then suddenly, a shift, a deviation; a random change of direction as an unexpected obstacle looms up, making the easy downward flow alter its course. It seems haphazard, but it isn't. The obstacle is there for a reason. The stream does not know why it's there or how the obstacle came to be in the way, but there it is, and it must be navigated.

Success! The resilient water finds the best route around, over, or through the offending obstacles and soldiers on to its destination. Where is that place? What will it look like? Will there be more obstacles, or is the path now clear and straightforward?

The descent slows for a bit, and the stream meanders along with no obvious route to its wanderings. It moves from here to there, around that rock, over that fallen branch, gurgling and swirling as little rocks, sticks and leaves beneath the surface shape its route. The path may be rocky and tricky to navigate, but there is such beauty in the journey if one can take a bit of time to see it. The water plays its gently flowing, or at times, powerful rushing music as it dances over, around, and through those things that lie in its path. That is lovely.

The stream may stay in this slow, meandering space for a bit, almost as if resting for what lies ahead. There is peace and rest here; deep pools reflect prisms of light as the sun filters through pine-scented branches. Small bugs dart about on their own journeys, busy and focused. Animals stop by for some refreshment, leaving their footprints in the soft, pungent soil, adding to or taking from the stream; the dance of life. Connection.

Eventually, the stream picks up speed, and the time for calm is over. Heading down the mountain, it rushes head-on into boulders, large fallen trees, and other forest-y things that would like to block its way. The pull of its destination forces the water to find a way over, around, through, and it does; it always does. It may be wild, gushing, and completely chaotic or slow, methodical, and plodding. But it will always reach its destination. The way has been charted out for this stream before it even existed. I picture my life in this way. I relate to the stream and the obstacles it must overcome, along with the times of rest and meandering, lazy peace. We all have a destination, and we will all reach it. My destination is the eternal arms of Jesus.

Mountain Path

MEANDERING OFF into the distance, the mountain path looks inviting.

Relaxed and lazy; where does it lead? Who has walked here before?

How many stories this lonely path must hold; what are its mysteries?

Warm sun complements the cool mountain breeze; perfect weather to explore!

Curiosity piqued; I set out with rocks and leaves crunching underfoot.

The silence is alive with nature doing its thing. Birds call out with their beautifully intricate songs; joyful and bright, full of energy.

Wildflowers dip and nod in the breeze, dancing to their own tune along the low, gentle hills.

Vibrant colors are splashed about in hues of blue, yellow, deep red-orange, a Divine paintbrush at work.

Busy insects hover and flit, carrying out the business of nature.

Mountain silence is full of life, purpose, and order, energizing yet calming.

I hear forest creatures rustling in bushes, peeking and darting.

Small animals are busy yet wary, alert, yet free in their mountain homes.

I wonder how many eyes are watching my progress along the path.

The air smells of warm earth and the faint perfume of wildflowers and sunshine.

Ascending at an easy pace, the land dotted with trees; the forest grows thicker.

A subtle change of light with deepening shades of green; a peaceful energy.

Dappled sunlight filters through treetops; birds soar from branch to branch, still calling.

The path feels springy underfoot, with a bed of needles and leaves covering the hard dirt.

Cooler air carries scents of pine and a not unpleasant older smell; moldy, ancient, circle of life.

Patches of wildflowers stubbornly crowd into pockets of sun that reach the forest floor.

Shots of bright beauty in the more subdued light, tenacious and bold!

In the distance, a loud crash through the underbrush; a deer, squirrels, a dead branch fallen?

Deeper in the woods, wind in the treetops mimic the susur-rating sigh of the sea; branches waving and swaying; stirring the calm air in a dance as old as time.

Walking deeper in, the trees are very close; sunlight is tightly filtered, and shadows play over the towering trunks as the path soldiers on.

Remote peace settles over the path, interrupted only by chattering squirrels and the noisy jay, demanding attention.

The air is quite cool. It smells crisp and deep, so clean and pure. Deep breaths to capture that scent memory forever.

Sun is dipping lower, a little farther, then time to turn back. Shadows deepen as the day ends. The scents, sights, and sounds are etched into memory. Captured.

Not making it to the very end of this mountain path, the mystery of it calls out to me. Keep going! Solve the mystery...

Maybe it was never meant to be fully known.

Look to the Clouds

THE SUMMER MORNING is warm with a brilliant, robin-egg blue sky. The warm dirt under my young back is soft yet bumpy with divots, small rocks, and tamped-down grasses. It smells comforting, earthy, and old. It feels safe.

The air is warm, and a bit close, broken up by the occasional snippet of breeze that lazily puffs over me in my earthy spot; grasses and wildflowers tossing and bobbing as the breeze slips through them, forcing movement on this indolent summer morning.

I fancy myself a cat; lazy, snooze-y, and hidden from view, yet spying and aware of all that is going on around my little nest.

There is a blue jay, raucous and naughty, dipping and darting as she looks for her breakfast in the oak trees. She is not afraid of disturbing the more stately robins and sparrows seeking out their morning meals. The birds do not notice me in my lair and continue their morning business, or maybe they do…

A variety of ducks and some Canadian geese glide by on the rippled water of the canal just a few feet away from me; blackberry brambles and other sticker bushes guard its banks like stubborn sentries. You can get through to the water if you dare to pass through them. Brave creatures have carved paths under and through these sentries, making their way to the water and safety. Their dens are cozy and well protected—easy access to tiny fish, frogs, and maybe crawdads.

Ah! There is the distinctive splash of the muskrat slipping through the cloudy waters of the canal. His path can be traced by following his bubbles as he searches below the waters for his breakfast. Routine. Safe. Ordinary.

Looking to the sky from my child-sized hollow in the summer faded grasses, I notice the white, marshmallow-like clouds floating past. They are fascinating! Some are huge and billowy, while others are small, wispy, and seem to vanish and meld into the bigger clouds nearby as if swallowed up.

Imagination has free reign while cloud watching. My mind can wander and make up all sorts of fantastical stories. I see one cloud that, at first glance, is just big, fluffy, and non-descript, but then it emerges; a boat with a crooked, tilted mast and a scraggly, wispy sail. Peeking over the side of the boat is a horse's head and a strange-looking bird. What stories that boat shall tell! Another cloud is almost perfectly round, except for one edge with a thin, feathery tail wafting off to the right, like a child's balloon rushing off in the wind on exciting adventures.

Breaking up the daydreams, the sleek, black cat saunters into my grassy hideout, curious and nosey, casually attacking a random leaf, sniffing around my hideaway, demanding pets and chin scratches. Having determined a spot near my head as acceptable, she settles in for a drowsy rest, as the warm morning is becoming a hot, summer afternoon. The shade is moving with the shifting sun, flooding my little earth-nest with a bit too much heat and light. Maybe it's time to get the sprinklers out as another dreamy, lazy, hot, Northern California summer day plods along into the next one.

Summer as a child was pleasant and predictable with routine, yet full of adventure by the canal behind my house. Lovely memories of feeding ducks and meeting the new ducklings, picking blackberries to make pies, cobblers, and jams, and taking long walks along the grassy, wildflower-laden paths near the canal bank. It felt joyful, exciting, new, yet familiar, and safe in that familiarity.

As an adult, I recapture bits and pieces of those childhood feelings when I revisit the canal with all its creatures, scents, and sounds. From the patio swing or the bench under the old oak with the blue wind chime I observe the ducks, geese, river otters and muskrats going about their business. The familiarity soothes and calms.

Tilting my head back to feel the sun, I allow the warmth to penetrate and loosen the chilled, hardened, practical places my adult mind has created. Sometimes life forces that on us, just to survive its onslaughts. Peering up through the gnarled, old branches of the oak tree, I see clouds. Puffed, billowing, white clouds, and I remember my child-self lying in the tall, warm grasses, surrounded by the stout wildflowers and nosey cats. Content and carefree. I remember the daydreams and simple joy of seeing life, nature, and me in the cloud shapes, imagining the Creator with His paintbrush, delighting me with adventures, and laughing as each stroke of His brush changed everything. There is peace and contentment for an exhausted, stressed, adult mind when I simply look to the clouds and allow that child-like joy and imagination to have its way for a bit and laugh with my Creator as He fills the sky with Himself.

Camping in the Woods

THERE IS NOTHING like the smell of the woods! Earthy and old, all-knowing, and rich. Divine creation.

Deep inhalation floods the senses with all sorts of stimulation and primal memories, life, connection, and ancient Earth rhythms. There is something nourishing here that feeds the soul, rejuvenating, expansive, and elemental. Back to our roots. The canvas camp chair nestled under a giant Redwood beckons, "Come, sit, be!"

The pace of these old, wise trees slows the heart and busy mind; infuses stillness and awareness and a sense of restful calm.

Looking up, I see the forever journey upward of these majestic trees, always yearning and following their source of Life—the Light. But not in a helter-skelter, chaotic way. The trees are stately, purposeful, and fierce in their growth. Some have grown around, over, under, or through whatever obstacles keep them from their Source. They know how to get there and do it unwaveringly, without frantic attempts and harebrained scheming. There is a lesson here in the trees for me. I feel it in my bones.

Life in the woods, on the surface, can seem frenetic, but a deeper, more careful look reveals the opposite. The birds, squirrels, raccoons, and other scurriers, big and small, are quite organized and methodical in how they go about their Creator-given tasks. Humbling. Teachable. Complete trust. My Creator has given me a specific task. Am I frantic in the doing?

If one is truly quiet, one can hear Nature doing its nature thing; cracks and snaps of branches bowing under the weight of a naughty, scolding jay; the tiny rustle of a fern frond, as an invisible creature makes its way on a well-worn path; the sibilant splash of a stream flowing from its source high above—who knows what adventures it experienced on its way downstream. The imagination can run wild here!

Dusk deepens in the woods, and Nature's life sounds change from the busy afternoon. There is a shift in the light and the night dwellers begin venturing out with different calls and purposes as the daytimers wind down and begin their settling in. Perfect rhythm. All in alignment.

Time for a campfire!

Sticks, dried leaves, and moss from the forest floor make a perfect bed for the larger sticks and logs to rest upon. Fire! Slowly it ignites and consumes the small sticks and random pieces of detritus that were thrown in the fire ring. The fledgling fire is mesmerizing as flames lick, snap, and dart through the wood, finding the best route and igniting all in its path.

The warmth and the crackling, snapping, and popping sounds recall happy memories of camping trips gone by; of long hikes and fishing, stories, and laughter by the fire late into the night, or of simple, quiet evenings of lulled conversation and companionable silence, as each one is captivated by the warmth and mystery of fire.

The forest is just as active at night as it is by day, but one must listen carefully and purposefully to know it. Nocturnal hunters, prowlers, and the curious are going about their business. I wonder what they think as they watch us, undetected, from the dark woods. Sleep beckons, so off to bed, soothed to sleep by the living forest.

Morning comes very early in the woods. Creatures up early to welcome the new day and begin their Creator-given work again. Bird calls sound joyful and insistent as day breaks. "Up, up, up!" They seem to shout. Nothing is wasted; every minute important in its own way, because this is survival. This is life.

So again, begins another day camping in the woods. The adventures are endless, and so are the lessons.

Walk in the Park

I LOVE how the autumn light filters and dances through the red and gold leaves; a light, pixie-like breeze gently rustling them, sending a few floating lazily to the ground.

Standing still for a moment, taking in the smell, the light, the feel of that breeze lightly brushing my skin, I feel my shoulders relax and drop down a bit as I smile and breathe deeply.

The packed dirt and gravel path look so inviting; it's already claimed other nature-loving souls this morning who heeded the call to get out and be refreshed; joggers, walkers, meanderers; their faces reflecting the serenity that I'm desperate for today.

Preoccupied squirrels with fluffy brown tails are busy with their autumn tasks, digging, ruffling, and burying their treasures. They make me happy. Oddly, it is calming and peaceful to see them hard at work yet seeming to revel in the autumn air and changing season as much as I am; their purposeful movements interspersed with dramatic bouts of scampering, scolding, and tail waving.

The crunch of small rocks and dried leaves makes a pleasing sound as I walk the park. Haphazardly scattered along the pathway, among the rocks and sticks and other seasonal detritus, I am delighted to find bright red and orange leaves, which at first sight seem random, yet cause me to marvel at Mother Nature and the seemingly perfect placement of her handiwork. Lovely. A bright spot on the path, a reminder to be alert and observe.

What else might I be missing? I still my mind and watch and listen and smell; I observe with eyes looking for small joys and beauty; the things so ordinary they are overlooked, yet packed with meaning, novelty, and beauty. Laughter. I hear it. Toddlers so delighted with their game of hide and seek that they shriek out their joy and reveal their hiding spaces, feeling confident and protected as they run full speed through the grass, filling their young lungs with air and collapsing in a giggling heap with their gasping parents close behind. This. This is living. Exhausting oneself with pure happiness!

There is the man on the shady bench with his dog; a picture of contentment as he strokes the white head of his poodle and talks gently to it. His face is serene, and his posture relaxed; the dog lying still observing us walkers, joggers, and meanderers. Easy companionship.

I see the determined jogger, who runs past with heavy breathing and intense focus on her path, yet takes a moment to make eye contact, smile, and chuff out a hello! Determined, yet aware.

From one vantage point at the far end of the path, I see the entire park open in front of me. I feel joyful. I can't help but smile wide at the deep green of the grassy area, where delighted dogs romp and chase far-flung Frisbees, frisking around their guardians. An older couple strolls hand in hand, taking in the park and all its beauty, totally unhurried. The mix of pines, oaks, and other trees offer shade and respite for those enjoying the morning. The playground is full of excited children busy at play, imagining themselves invincible as they climb the slide ladder.

This walk in the park helped me shed a feeling of heaviness I did not realize I had been carrying. I feel relaxed, open, and light, aware of just how much the ordinary is designed to bring joy, peace, and a sense of centering, but we must have our senses ready to receive it. Our Creator knew what He was up to, down to every slight detail; so intricate, yet so often overlooked, as we search out something huge and wild and shattering to bring back our peace and our sense of normalcy, when all we need is right in front of us, waiting to be seen with new eyes and fresh appreciation. Nature is calling; can you hear her?

Autumn

We lovers of Autumn have a sixth sense about us, a knowing when that first revelation of summer's end has arrived.

It is felt on the skin in that barely discernable nip and twinge of air, charged with the slightest chill; awareness that the atmosphere has changed just a smidge.

Autumn's scent is unique and mischievous. Earthy and deep; wise, pungent, and bold in the way brown leaf tips, restless trees, and fading flowers bend and drop to the Earth, daring the one watching to stop them; to impede the ancient progress of a slow, yet lovely descent into quiet and rest.

That spritely spurt of wind, which tosses and dances fallen leaves and finished flowers round and round, is delightful. What is it about piling up crispy, browned leaves then dashing them about, flinging them from orderly piles into random and untamed flurries of color? A new beginning; a tossing and mixing up of the old, lazy routine into something new; a plan to disrupt the status quo and wait patiently through the winter, as that plan takes form and substance. Somehow the chaos of it is lovely and energizing, part of the ritual. It is one more wild streak before the settling and simmering of autumn moves on to the mystery and silent brooding of winter.

The discerning observer will witness Nature's response to the shift from the indolent, dog days of summer to autumn's call to let go. The song of quiet purpose and intention, as Mother Earth whispers it's time to fold in, cozy up, and allow rest to perform its miracles and the deep, sweet slumber of winter to wait in the wings.

There is something inspiring and invigorating in this call to purposeful letting go, an anticipation. Is it the definitive color changes and that unmatched fall scent in the air that feels like a new beginning? Is it the crisp sensation of fall air as one breathes it in?

Welcome Autumn! Come and show off your colors and dare us to think about the dead or dying places that we need to let fall; not with sadness or fear; but with anticipation that a season of silent regrouping, where new life starts to bud, will soon break free with the coming of spring. It's coming, and it will be glorious!

The Lake

THE PATH around the lake is a bit overgrown but navigable. I wonder whose feet last hiked this trail. What were they hoping to find here at the lake, nestled in the mountain meadows?

This path is not new; scuff marks from countless boots have worn a soft pathway in the alpine meadow, gently leading around the blue-green water of the lake. I am alone here with the only sounds being my feet, as they lead me to my favorite spot, and nature, doing its thing. Birds call and snicker to each other as I pass by, dipping and darting over the water as they snip up the buzzing, whirring insects that make the lake and tall grasses their home. Parts of the path are cool and shady, winding along under the forest canopy, then sneaking out into the open meadow with wildflowers nodding and swaying as the breeze passes through, sighing through the canopy, and stirring my hair.

The banks of the lake are home to such diverse life, with the nooks and hollows filled with myriad water skippers, boatmen, pollywogs, and tiny fish darting and spying as I lean down to get a closer look. How can one lake hold the life of so many creatures and plants in its watery, silty hands? Carefully kneeling, I notice the lake rushes rustle and shiver as a creature makes its way through the slippery murk at the edge of the lake. It is totally immersed in the tall, wet grasses; hunting, watching, doing what it was meant to do. Is it a muskrat? I become as still as I can and quietly watch and wait...then yes, I see its long brown body gracefully dip underwater. Bubbles breaking on the lake's surface give away how swift he can swim as he heads to his den on the lake bank. I have a feeling I will be carefully watched.

Moving again, I pass a cold and deep-looking spot right along the edge of the lake. There is a long since fallen pine tree along the banks, and I wonder what fish may live in that deeper, dark part. Has a fellow hiker ever tried to cast her fishing line in, hoping to hook a big trout? Looking carefully around the fallen pine, I notice a shallow area with sunlight filtering through the trees and spot a large crawdad, its orangey-red pincher motionless. Has it spotted me? Finding a long, slim stick, I gently submerge the tip and try to touch that claw. It is too fast for me and darts under part of the fallen pine. I smile and tell it I am sorry for disturbing its rest and move along the path.

My destination is coming up. Just a few more twisty turns, under a low hanging branch and over some high raised roots, and I am there. My spot is at the edge of the meadow that curves and moves along the edges of the lake. There is a sweet little mountain stream that winds its way down the slopes and forest floor and feeds into this lake. I love this place the most.

Swinging off my light backpack, I bring out what I need to get comfy. A thick blanket, water, some vittles, and my book that probably will not be cracked open. The blanket is large enough to accommodate the various positions I may choose as I sit, lie, stretch, and soak up my spot. The babbling chatter of the stream as it flows, dips, and rushes past forest debris, rocks, and flowering plants make me happy. It is cheerful, chatty, and constant yet completely soothes and refreshes my tired soul as it chips away the debris of life. It leaves a tender, slightly raw place inside which revels in the solitude of nature, babbling streams, throaty frogs, and cricket symphonies; gossipy, scolding birds, slithery, earthy sounds, and the busy, buzzing sounds of insects. And the smells, oh the smells! Earthy, fresh, and that distinctive lake smell—part mud, part plant, part fishy, part flowers and pine. It smells new yet ancient all at once, and it is lovely.

I have the afternoon ahead of me to be still, listen, daydream, and let some of the heaviness go. I have needed this for a while. I am ready to soak in whatever the Creator has for me here by the lake. My mind wanders to Psalm 23, "...He lets me rest in green meadows; He leads me beside peaceful streams. He renews my strength." Renewal. Yes.

My day at the lake is ending. The wind has begun to sigh and whisper through the trees, as it will in the afternoons. My signal that the sun is starting its trek to the west, and sunset will soon be here. Packing up, I take another long look at the stream and lake, drinking in that afternoon of peace and restoration. Heading back along the trail, I smile and speak aloud this renewal and peace, "It is well, it is well, with my soul!"

The Old Barn

I GLIMPSE IT from the country road. It's down the next gentle curve, off on a little-used side road, possibly forgotten; full of ruts, some potholes, and waving, faded wildflowers; abandoned yet peaceful. This calls to me. So beautiful.

Turning off the road, I follow the pocked and tumbled lane, carefully maneuvering, following the faded track to the old, falling-down barn. It's graceful and lovely. There is history here. Stories abound within these wind and weather scoured timbers. I need to see it, feel it, breathe it in.

Pulling off the jutted lane, I stop the car, quietly get out and just stand a minute. Absorbing, listening, watching. The silence begins to speak, and it is a beautiful language, the silence. I know it well, and it feels like a comfortable old quilt; old, wise, full of life, and so many possibilities. It has so much to say, and the wisdom—the wisdom gained from silence is not lost on me.

To the left of the ramshackle barn, an old oak tree still casts shade and shadows; it has weathered much. A thick, frayed rope swings lightly in the breeze. Maybe a tire swing hung there, propelling its riders on so many adventures, the freedom of flight!

A birdhouse tacked to the upper part of the old oak has seen better days. Part of the tiny roof is missing, and something has gnawed a small hole in the floor of it. Someone, a child perhaps, painted a welcome sign above the bitty door to the birdhouse. Welcome Home, it says, in faded orange paint. Closing my eyes, I see and hear the many families this old house has sheltered through the years. Mamas and babies and the first tentative attempts at flight; the swooping, diving, bug catching, and seed collecting. Nature doing its thing in a never-ending cycle.

Standing in the silence, I hear a cheeky giggling, bubbling coming from the other side of the barn. A creek! Gingerly making my way, I brush through tall meadow grasses and an assortment of wildflowers that have claimed the long-forgotten space. The happy water-sounds call to me. I find the creek and simply watch for a bit, listening and observing. I don't know the origin of this pretty creek. It snakes through the gentle rises and falls of this land, making its way to the destination meant for it. It is not daunted by obstacles. It goes over, under, or around as it can; it always finds a way, and there is always a path for it—an endpoint. I wonder if it knows that it carries so much life in its twists and turns and frothy bubbling. On the quieter edges, I see tiny fish gathering in the sunny spots and darting away as my shadow falls on them. I think I see a crawdad, and I hear a woodpecker hammering on the old oak. I spend some time here by this creek. The joy in the nature-chatter of it makes me feel happy and somehow ancient and in tune with Mother Earth.

The abandoned barn still beckons, and I respond. I imagine it in its heyday. I think it was a reddish color, but it is so weathered, and sun and wind burned that its exact color is hard to determine. How proud it must have looked when it was first erected! I picture pickup trucks full of neighbors and wood and nails, helping build it. The lively shouts and laughter as they worked together must have been comforting and friendly. Was there a barn raising party here after the work was done? It's big enough inside that I envision a long trestle table filled with vittles and cold lemonade and ice water. Comradery. A life lived and protected under the timbers and beams.

A rusted old pitchfork is leaning jauntily against what looks like an old stall. Did a horse live here? The railings are falling, and a couple are broken and jagged. Further in, old, withered ropes are looped on lichen-covered hooks, and a broken-down wheelbarrow sits. There is a remnant of loft beams overhead, long tumbled, and rickety. A hole in the roof speaks of heavy snows that over the years weakened and dashed the beams. How lovely, quiet, and breath-taking this barn must be, covered in the powdery white of a snowfall. I will be back to see that.

Large tufts of grasses, a ripped old sack, and abandoned hay look to be patted down in the left side corner of the old barn. A creature finds shelter here, warm and safe, despite the battered look of this old barn. Looks are deceiving. The barn's skeleton and frame are still useful and needed. Life is still very much present here. I find that comforting. The outer glory and flash of this barn may be diminished, but it still shelters. It is still needed but in a quieter and gentler way. Roof beams directly above me have been claimed as home by birds. I can see the nests, abandoned now but ready for the return of nature, all in its perfect timing.

The large, half-cracked open door at the back of the barn hangs on dilapidated hinges that have their fair share of rust; parts of them just holes, eaten through by time, wind, heat. I carefully make my way to that door. On the side beam that forms the support for the door is the name Jill, written in squiggly, nail-cut writing. There is a heart, a cat, and a smiley face etched nearby. This barn had stories, and adventures lived out inside its walls. I wonder if Jill told this old barn her secrets; are they contained in the walls and the beams?

The wind picks up a bit, and through the chinks and cracks, it whispers and sighs. Its breath is new and fresh, yet has all the undercurrents of time passed, secrets and hints of the supernatural, the Divine. The old and ancient, ramshackle, and run-down have so much to teach us. Nothing is entirely as it seems on first look. What appears abandoned and useless often carries far more than the passing glance reveals. Life needs the old things. Cracked and weathered beams still protect and teach and shelter. There are safe, soft corners that can be missed if overlooked.

A squirrel chatters nearby, and a bird trills and scolds. I give another look and listen to the old barn. It is time to go. I won't soon forget this old barn. What a welcome detour it has been, this reconnection to the silence and healing of the old, time-worn, and abandoned. "Thank you," I tell it. "I will be back."

...in chaos

Death of a Stronghold

I WANT out of here. I am so cold. It's getting darker. Where did the light go? The air feels heavy and oppressive. It's getting harder to breathe. I can hardly see anything around me. I reach out my hands to grasp the door. My fingers brush across the handle, but it doesn't budge. I've been sealed in. Heavy, awkward-looking blocks are stacked in front of the door, seemingly tossed in random piles but effectively blocking my escape. "Who did this?" I wonder. I turn around, surveying this place I've built for myself. Funny, I don't remember it looking so bare, empty, and void of life, like a grave. There is nothing of me in this place. What happened here?

I try to remember the last time I saw it as it used to be—strong, safe, impenetrable, guarding my secrets. It was a long time ago. I allow my eyes to wander around the room, and then I see them. The boxes...a flicker of recognition snatches at my thoughts, and the old feelings of terror and pain stir and begin to move toward the surface. I see memories shimmering inside their tightly-bound boxes where I banished them all that time ago. "No, no," I cry, "I can't! I can't see you!" Not yet... not yet...

My heart is pounding. "I can't; please don't make me." I am frozen, staring at the memories bumping up against the lids of the boxes, straining against the ropes I used to tightly bind them away out of sight. They have been safely tucked away in this tower of heavy blocks I constructed for them. I worked so hard.

I can't look at them. I am too afraid. Then, in the silence, almost imperceptibly, I feel the air stir, like the faintest breeze, buoyant, like a soft feather dancing lightly against my bare skin. I catch the scent of something wonderful! It smells new, clean, and light. Pure. I know this scent but can't yet place it; it's been so long since I've breathed it in.

In contrast, the stench of death, decay, and emptiness in this place is overwhelming yet cloying and familiar. My imprisoned soul is drawn to the new, the clean, the light, and I search for its origin. Compelled by something supernatural, completely unexplainable, I move toward the boxes. I am right there, closer to them than I have been in ages. Despite the desperate sinuous fear crowding me on all sides, I sense a shift in the air. It is lighter, and I don't feel crushed by the weight of it. I smell the beautiful scent again, and it gives me courage. There is a palpable change in the atmosphere now. I feel the gentle, sweet brush of feathers all around me and know I am safe. I slowly let myself be drawn in again. The stench of death and decay is very faint now, replaced by the scent of Heaven coming from the wings and feathers in which I find myself enfolded. Your voice is huge, powerful, deep, yet gentle, quiet, and sure.

"It is time. Look at them now, child; open your boxes."

"Only if You promise to stay. I cannot face them alone," I whisper.

Strength flows into me that I know cannot be of me. I am all too familiar with the sense of my own failed strength. Your voice reverberates through the very core of my being, saying, "I alone am your refuge; your place of safety; I am your God, and you will trust Me. I will shield you with My wings; I will shelter you with My feathers. My faithful promises are your armor and protection."

Yes, Father, yes.

You place the frayed, weathered ropes that bind up my boxes of memories into my right hand. I still have Your strength flowing through me, so I pull the ropes with all my might. As the ropes slither to the ground, my memories, carefully hidden and preserved, gently dance and hover above the box tops, bidding me to look at them and release them. A peace that I cannot understand washes over me, and I go to the boxes.

Your hand warm upon my head; feathers brushing my cheeks. I inhale You and deeply breathe in Life. I lift my head and welcome the memories, and they come. I look at each one as they come before me. I weep and cry out as I acknowledge them all; the violence, terror, pain, and fear; the cruel words and hateful actions, and slowly nod my head. I feel You hold me tight and whisper to my spirit. I am startled and struck silent as I feel the sweet warmth of Your tears spill onto my face as You weep for me. You turn my face upwards, and I watch my memories, my pain, my loss ascending to Heaven, where You will take them and re-shape them to be used for Your glory. "Is it done, Father?" I ask.

"What about these walls of heavy blocks you constructed to protect your pain? Is it not time to tear that down, too, Daughter? Do you really want to be free?" You take my hands and turn them over. They are calloused and rough from all those exhausting years of building my stronghold. I watch in awe as Your breath, and Your right hand begin to smooth away the hardness, deep grooves, and scales, revealing new skin underneath that glows with life, energy, and health. New life is here; in this place seeped in death and emptiness.

In the next moment, my attention is caught by a sound unlike anything I have ever heard before. It starts as a deep, low rushing, and then begins to spiral upwards, like a roar, like a violent storm, and I fear I can't stand up under the enormity of it. It is too much for me to bear, and I close my eyes, barely breathing. As quickly as it came, it is gone. There is peace, blessed silence, as I rest safely in the shadow of Your wings. The roar is replaced by the most beautiful song I have ever heard, being sung above me, all around me. I cannot understand the words being spoken; it is too lofty for me, but something deep in my spirit awakens and responds. I am utterly captivated. I feel so light, so new, so clean!

As I raise my arms in praise and abandon, I see that I am free! The walls I built are no more, the boxes are gone, the air is clean, and the light is back. Gingerly, I begin walking where once the walls of my self-imposed prison stood tall. I notice only a slight indentation, like a scar, left there, indicating where the pit of my captivity had once been. Today is the day I traded my stronghold for a strong tower. As I soak in the song You sing over me, Your voice becomes imprinted on my heart, "I am the Lord Your God, I am with you, I am mighty to save. I will take great delight in you; I will quiet you with My love, I will rejoice over you with singing."

A Divine Exchange

MAYBE THIS TIME, I tell myself. I can do it. I'm strong, and I can handle this. I strain to see. I try to remember how it looks, but it's been a long time. A primal knowledge in my soul tells me that I need to see it, must find it again, but things are obscured through the webs; my vision seems cloudy, and I can't make out the shapes in the strangely filtered light. Frustration wells up as the heaviness settles back in to take the place I've given it.

When did that happen? Did I give it permission? I used to hear, but the sounds I'm searching for are muffled now, faint and far off, disturbed by an odd rattling and scraping. Frustration, blindness, and confusion; is this where I've settled? "Maybe if I move around, I can get a better view," I decide.

With that decision made, I stand and am confronted with the source of the rattling, scraping sounds; thick, heavy, rusted chains. My chains. Mine. I can't get up and move around for a better view because I am bound to this place of filtered light, muffled sounds, and intolerable frustration. Why? When? How? Panicked, I struggle and fight, then, in exhaustion, slump down in defeat. Tears fall from my eyes and splatter down on the ground. Am I bound here forever? Is there no escape? Dark images flicker, and stealthy movements threaten and mock. Is that faint laughter I hear? I didn't start out here, bound like this, in chains like a condemned prisoner. Who put me here? What did I do? "Please," I call out, "someone, will you help me?" I don't belong here. I want out. "Someone, rescue me!"

I hear faint movement coming from all around me. The dark shapes are shrouded by the obscure, filtered light, but I sense them coming closer, bold and violent, mocking in their approach. "Help yourself," one hisses in my ear, arrogance and fear scenting its breath, mocking laughter flowing from its tongue. As hopelessness starts to fall, I look more closely at my surroundings. I am elevated on a mass of circular stones with faded words written on each one. They are carefully arranged and set just so in a small clearing, like an altar. All beauty has been methodically wiped away, revealing only dust, barrenness, and grotesquely twisted roots, thrusting up out of the ground. The harsh loneliness of this place is terrifying.

Wait…I can see more clearly now; this used to be shadow-like and obscure, but now I sense the light shifting; brighter, clearer, full. I don't like what I see. Webs from something horrid and smothering have been woven around, above, and below my prison, trapping me, altering my view, skewing my perspective. "Lies," a Voice gently says, "lies that have kept you snugly ensconced on your altar of self." Altar of self. Yes, that is exactly what this is. As recognition of my pridefully built, self-imposed prison floods my awareness, I realize that I cannot get out on my own. I have locked myself in. Trapped. The mocking laughter swells, and I feel the heaviness trying to descend again, the weight of my chains pulling cruelly at my limbs.

"ENOUGH!" I shout. "Please, Jesus, You have the keys to set me free!"

The mocking laughter is silenced by my words. The atmosphere shifts and grows completely still, except for a deep vibration surging up from the altar as it cracks in two. A clear stream of water gushes out from the crack. You stoop down and scoop the water in Your hands and offer it to me. I see the silvery scars on Your hands, and a song I can't name but deeply understand floods my soul—thirst-quenching. A divine exchange is taking place here, and my cracked altar becomes the catalyst.

The sounds and scents I have longed for reach me. Sweet laughter, gentle voices, Spirit breath, heavenly song. Delicate and powerful, they flow around me, bathing me in sounds and scents so sweet and pure that my breath comes in gasps, expelling the dust and debris that accumulated in my spirit as I worshipped at the altar of self.

I breathe You in deeply, richly, slowly. Freedom bathes me, ministering to the wounds inflicted by the stones named Fear, Pain, Loneliness, Pride, Rebellion, and Abuse that I used to build my altar. I feel lighter, clean, loved. Heavy, rusted chains break apart and fall away from me. I dance before you with abandon, unashamed, cleansed, my weakened muscles growing stronger and nimbler. The heaviness is gone, and a gentle, vibrant spirit of praise now clothes me.

"Climb down, child, get down off your broken altar. Take the stones with you; they have a purpose to fulfill here. There is something you need to see again." I fill my white robe with all those stones. Somehow, they all fit. I follow You out of the clearing where the altar once stood. As I go, new life is sprouting up. The gnarled roots of bitterness and rage, rejection, and vengeance sprout into lovely trees of forgiveness, peace, Sonship, and humility.

"Stop here, beloved; you must use these stones to build your steps leading up to My Cross." I look at the Cross, and it speaks of ultimate sacrifice, profound mercy, joy indescribable, unmatched beauty, and plentiful grace, even grace for one who built her own altar of self-protection. Tears of gratitude wash over my face and spill down onto my hands as I build those steps. It is hard work. My building stops at times as I find a tenacious tendril of frustration or pride trying to creep in over my stones, but I rip it out with Your strength in my hands. As I lift my stones into place, I notice that where my tears have fallen, shoots of brilliant green push their way out of the rich soil. As the sprouts emerge, You bend down and write something on the ground and speak tenderly to the new sprouts. Your voice is the nourishment they need. You rejoice over the harvest that only You can see.

My steps are built. They are placed firmly and deeply into the ground at the foot of Your Cross. Engraved by Your hand on that first step are the words Nisi Dominus Frustra. "Come up, Daughter. Come up higher to the very foot and find rest. Here is what you have been searching for in vain."

I ascend those steps in anticipation. As I come closer, I stop and look down, surveying where I started. My tears watered what You divinely planted, and I see beauty stretching out below me, and Your Cross is beauty before me. I feel a shout that I cannot contain rising in my throat, so I shout! It is a shout of pure joy, a song from my spirit to Yours. A harvest will be reaped from my pain that I never thought I had a right to know. It is a beautiful inheritance. It is You.

Places in the Heart

THERE ARE many hiding places in the heart. There are compartments, dark corners, nooks, and crannies. Compartments come in many shapes and sizes. They often contain to-do lists, work details, holiday plans, and the like. These compartments are easy to access. They are typically pleasant, if not monotonous, places to visit. The dark corners, nooks, and crannies are less friendly. Sometimes dusty and unkempt, these places in the heart hold memories; some pleasant, some preferred to be forgotten, or some softened with age, but still revisited occasionally for nostalgia's sake. Sometimes these nooks and crannies hold things that caused embarrassment, shame, and guilt that we shelved away in boxes and were quickly forgotten. Maybe situations that were not resolved to our liking are stored here, to be resurrected and stewed over again and again. These places can usually be safely revisited and forgiven, even laughed at once the sting is gone.

However, carefully tucked away in a little-visited corridor of the soul is the heavily locked door, maybe many doors. These doors are toxic and forbidden. The corridors leading to them are oftentimes lined with traps, snares, and distractions to keep the unwanted visitor out, to protect, control, and deny entrance. If somehow the corridor is navigated and the traps avoided, the doors themselves are well armored to repel intruders. Thick and impenetrable, ugly, and seeping, these doors are repulsive with a cloying scent of decay and primal fear. The keyholes are rusted with disuse, and the hinges are stuck shut.

Somewhere in a closed-off part of your heart, you sense that all is not well down there in the deep recesses of the soul. You do remember. You can navigate the traps and snares in the long-ignored passageways because you put them there. With a disconcerting sense of focus, you walk the corridor that leads to the forbidden places. You will control them. As you stand in front of your door in a rare surge of bravery, you unlock it and force the door to open. The heavy keys clink to the filthy ground as they fall from your fingers. An overwhelming sense of hopelessness, sickness, and fear blow past you, as the toxic, decay-filled air swirls, threatens, and mocks.

"You can't fix this," a voice whispers, "it is far too late." The boxes and bundles you see inside are angry, weeping wounds that none of your heavy bandaging seemed to stop. How long have you been bleeding like this? You worked so hard to cover, heal, and deal with these wounds! You bound them up tightly with the bonds of denial, saturated them with the balm of self-reliance, murmuring rote words of Christianese over them, willing them with your mind to stop seeping, stop oozing their filth. Yet somewhere far down, in your deepest soul, you know it didn't work. You are still bleeding.

You venture in through the door a bit further, taking in all the chaos and violence that is trapped here. The door slams shut. Darkness is overwhelming, and taunting voices grow louder, shouting that you have no way out and that these wounds will never heal. The loneliness is palpable, and despair is closing in, threatening to remove all hope. Yet above the din of raucous laughter, you hear it; faint at first, but growing stronger, louder, and more insistent. Someone is knocking on the closed door! You see light on the other side! Stumbling, tripping, falling, you wrench the door wide, and there on the threshold of your vile door is the Light! This Light is not repelled by the darkness, the seeping, and the stench. It dispels it.

"Here I am! I stand at the door and knock. If anyone hears my voice and opens the door, I will come in and eat with that person, and they with me."[1]

"Eat with me? In here? It is horrible, unsafe, and unclean," you say. "I'm too ashamed to let You enter into this place." The Light enters anyway, pushing through all the decay, fear, and chaos. As the Light passes by each of your weeping, oozing boxes, He stops and looks carefully and fully at all the damage wrapped up inside the haphazardly bandaged bundles. He sees it all. He never looks away. He sees every word, every action, and act of violence. He sees all the fear and hurt that created

---

1   Revelation 3:20

each wound. He acknowledges the pain and panic of all of it, and you begin to feel that heavy burden lift from your shoulders. He has taken it. He doesn't turn away from the ooze and mess. He doesn't look at your face with eyes of disgust and dismissal. Instead, the Light reaches into His robe of white and pulls out a lovely crystal bottle that shimmers and dances in the light of the Light. "These are your tears. I catch every single one. I rejoice over all of them because I turn them into your treasures."

He turns back to the boxes and bundles and begins to bind them up and heal them, one by one. The rags of denial are replaced with linens of pure white, the balm of self-reliance is wiped away, and in its place, the oil of gladness is massaged in, bringing hope and wholeness. As He works, songs and words of Heaven pour from His lips. Healing. When He is finished, the stench and ooze are gone, replaced with spicy scents of freshness that hint at renewal and rebirth. You see this once for-bidden, closed-off room as a renewed place of hope, testimony, and strength. There are crystal bottles lining the shelves where once your pain and secrets hid. In the center of your exposed and now beautiful room, you see a table is set, where you are invited to quench your hunger and thirst with the One who heals the brokenhearted and binds up their wounds. "Taste and see that the LORD is good; blessed is the one who takes refuge in him."[2]

---

2   Psalm 34:8

Communion with Heaven

"THOSE WHO LIVE in the shelter of the Most High will find rest in the shadow of the Almighty. This I declare of the Lord: He alone is my refuge, my place of safety; He is my God, and I am trusting in Him."[1]

I'm searching for shelter. Protection and rest seem elusive. There is too much noise, so much confusion. This landscape is dry, hot, and barren. I am weary. I found shelter, rest, and protection once upon a time. Somehow, bit by bit and small step by small step, I came out from the places of safety. Oh, it was very subtle, my wandering, slow and insouciant, without the purposeful intent of distancing myself and going too far, but nonetheless, I left my safe haven. It felt a little exhilarating to be out on my own, managing things; keeping things orderly and controlled. Venturing out from under the shady covering

---

1   Psalm 91: 1-2

seemed fine, well deserved. I felt stronger, and Your strength lifted me and gave me confidence.

"I am stronger," I said. "There are things I can do on my own."

"Watch yourself succeed," Self-Reliance whispered.

"You know you can, and so does He," Ego breathed.

"Trust yourself," Pride hissed in my ear. Well, only a little way out; I won't be gone long...

A little way turned out to be quite a journey. There were cheerful, encouraging voices urging me on, out into the unknown. "Go on!" they shouted. "You're free; show us what you're made of! You are needed out there!" Yes, yes, I am needed and have so much to offer.

Traveling on, I notice things are not so easy anymore; control is not coming willingly, and my knowledge and understanding are not adequate. My strength isn't enough, and I am weary, thirsty, and afraid. Anxiety and worry are like leeches that I cannot shake off. They dog me exhaustingly and relentlessly until there seems no way out from under the heavy weight I am carrying. I grow weaker under the pressure of it all. The once friendly, encouraging voices have changed their tune. Instead of cheers and words of praise, I hear mocking laughter so full of malice it is unbearable. The chaos that surrounds me sucks all peace and beauty from where I find myself. I am in a wasteland of my own making, and I cannot save myself. I am sure You must have abandoned me, left me to my own devices. Weariness overtakes me, and I have nothing left. Lowering my face to the ground, I feel something soft, lovely, and gentle, cushioning my cheek. I cry, asking You to come and rescue me.

You come. I sense a presence more glorious and breathtaking than anything I have ever known come over me. You are here. At your feet are angels, against whose wings I am resting my cheek. You are the most powerful, wild, and terrible yet beautiful vision I have ever seen! You stand above me with Your wings spread out over, above, and all around me, my refuge, and my fortress. Your eyes are closed, and I hear the song again! The song that You sang over me when Your mercy and love rescued me. Your eyes hold mine, and feelings of acceptance and worth pool and flow around my entire being. Bathed in Your mercy, washed in Your love. Shelter. Safety. I lie at Your feet feeling light, free, and at peace.

I am wanted. Your angels lift me up, and I sit at Your feet, looking back over the places I've been. I notice my wayward path. I can see where stones, traps, and snares were shoved away. Small pieces of feathery white show brightly against some of the larger rocks, where they were snagged as a way was made for me. "For He will order His angels to protect you wherever you go. They will hold you up with their hands so you won't even hurt your foot on a stone."[2] I was protected; even along the path I was not meant to walk.

"Watch, daughter," You say. Subtly, the air begins to stir, gently at first and then stronger and more violent. The atmosphere sizzles and snaps, and I am frozen to my spot under Your

---

2   Psalm 91: 11-12

wings. There is a commotion, a rupture of sorts, throwing me to my knees. It is terrifying. Something huge is shifting and rending the ground I am standing on, like a bringing down of giants. Strongholds. You are breaking them. It is chaos and destruction, but I am untouched. The wind and air are warm. There is enormous power at work here beyond anything I have ever witnessed.

Suddenly, I am lifted off my knees, and something slams into my body; it is supernatural, terrifyingly beautiful. A bright light explodes in my chest and eyes, and I feel so hot that I am numb. I can't breathe, but Your Spirit is breathing for me. I turn my face up to the sky, open my mouth, and sing. I sing with such force that I can feel my chest and throat thrumming. As I watch, my voice becomes a beam of white-blue light that points straight into Heaven. The sound of my singing is so beautiful. I have never heard anything like it. There are no words that I can understand, but the sounds are beyond description. As I sing, other voices join me that are even more beautiful and haunting than my own but blend beautifully, perfectly.

Deep is calling to deep, and I am part of it. I see it, feel it, hear it, and know it. A communion with Heaven. Then it fades and is gone. I am left completely spent, lying face down, trying to process in my finite mind what I was just blessed to witness. Sounds of peace and singing, scents of beauty brush over me, healing and filling the redeemed places with validation of Your love for me. I am wanted, not needed. I can trust you with me. Gingerly raising myself up, I see that I am no longer in a wasteland. I am in a place that is alive with hope, joy, and new life. Strongholds were broken this day. I have found rest.

"He who dwells in the shelter of the Most High will rest in the shadow of the Almighty...because He loves me," says the Lord. "I will rescue him; I will protect him, for he acknowledges my name. He will call upon me, and I will answer him. I will be with him in trouble; I will deliver him and honor him. With long life will I satisfy him and show him my salvation."[3]

---

3   Psalm 91: 1, 14-16

The Tapestry

THE WOOL THREADS display the richest colors as they flow across the loom, some vibrant and brilliant, which immediately draw the eye and capture attention, while other shades and hues are subdued, calming, and deep, visible only to those who truly see. The Master Weaver has been at His work forever, and He will not stop until it is completed. His breath creates and calls into existence that which was not into what is. His thoughts and His songs, His glance, and His robes are all part of the Divine dance that weave and blend to make a way where there wasn't one. Supernatural, unstoppable, beautiful.

We each have a unique tapestry. No tapestry is the same, yet our individual threads intersect, overlap, advance, and retreat as the tapestry is woven, and the Creator's plans come into being. What He sends forth will not return void. It will accomplish the exact and perfect purpose for which it was sent. Perfection. Mysterious. Holy.

I imagine an open space that is peaceful and joyful, where the Master does His creating. It is a place filled with pure, flowing water, incense, and beauty. It is called Holy Ground. This sacred spot is where the weaving happens. It is precious and well-guarded. There is joy, tender love, hurt, and tears. Laughter and grief intermingle and twine about each other in a dance that is gorgeous, fierce, completely untamed, terrifying, and yet carefully orchestrated. Who can contain and control what Heaven has spoken and breathed into life?

The individual tapestries stand alone, yet they do not. Each one is carefully and precisely ordered to intersect, surprise, and flow into the others. Each tapestry is necessary for the others to come to fruition. Certain tapestries will be woven together for a lifetime, others for a few moments, years, days, or seasons. Some may barely skim the borders of another, yet there is a Divine purpose for the skimming and the overlapping, the touching, and intersecting.

The Creator knows, and that is enough. He sees it for how it is, how it was, and He will see it long after we are called home. Perhaps we will see His master plan with unveiled eyes, once blurred from striving to understand, force, or remove these divine intersections. What is woven together can't be undone by the tapestry. Struggling is futile and distracts from the beauty unfolding minute by minute in front of us. No, we can't foresee, tame, and reverse that which was breathed by Holy breath into existence. This is where hope and faith must come into play.

There are lessons that must be learned, hurts healed, and other tapestries that need the colors, hues, and patterns the

Weaver chose to color your life tapestry. These will not always blend in perfect harmony. This mixture will, at times, appear chaotic and unsafe, as if they should not have been allowed to brush against each other. The Master Craftsman knows how it all unfolds because He saw it from the beginning. Alpha and Omega.

What appears as chaos, pain, and discord at the moment is part of the dance. He knows the steps because He created them. We can't pretend to understand the whys and purposes behind His plan, but one day I hope we will. When the final thread in our tapestry is woven, and the Weaver shepherds us into the place called Holy Ground, we will see how it all blends into something lovely, ordered, and precise, and we will stand in awe of it; smiling through tears of understanding as the height, breadth, and depth of His perfect love covers us. We will watch in fascination as the remaining tapestries are sung and danced over, breathed upon, and woven together until He leans back from His loom, declares it is finished, and brings His masterpieces home to be forever displayed in the Most Holy Place, for all of eternity.

...at the Feast

The Banner

"THE LORD is my shepherd; I shall not want. He makes me lie down in green pastures; He leads me beside quiet waters; He restores my soul. He guides me in paths of righteousness for His name's sake. Even though I walk through the valley of the shadow of death, I will fear no evil, for you are with me; your rod and your staff, they comfort me. You prepare a table before me in the presence of my enemies. You anoint my head with oil; my cup overflows. Surely goodness and love will follow me all the days of my life, and I will dwell in the house of the Lord forever."[1]

There is change in the air; I can feel it. I stand on a gentle rise and see the banner in the distance snapping boldly, vivid colors weaving and twisting in the steady breeze. It's been there, just beyond those high, craggy mountains, since the start of

---

1   Psalm 23

my journey with You, as a backdrop in a production. I feel very drawn to it, yet can't quite explain the pull it has on me. Something bright under that banner catches my eye. What is that glinting in the sunlight? I survey the path opening before me in the soft grass, wildflowers nodding and dipping as the perfumed air lifts and tosses them about on their slender green stems. Such beauty here; such peace—must I leave this place? Is it already time to move on?

Memories return of days spent resting and healing when time seemed to stand still as I walked with You by the quiet waters, drinking in Your presence as You restored my soul. My scars have begun to fade, pieces of my shattered soul returned to their rightful places, stronger than before. My mind and spirit are full of the sweet memory of grace and mercy poured out over me as strongholds fell and angels rejoiced over the victory. Strength has returned to bones made weary from battles only fully comprehended in the Heavenlies. You revealed a pathway of righteousness and truth, and my feet were set upon it, leading me to Your place of safety and rest.

I turn toward the sound of Your footsteps coming toward me, firm and strong. "Come, child," You say. "Today is the day."

"I'm not sure I'm ready yet, Father; I'm not fully healed. Please, can I rest just a bit longer?"

I notice Your staff in Your hand and turn to look again at the path before me. Level at first, it seems to ascend, and not too far off, I see the beginnings of hills, and further in the distance, the mountains; bigger than the ones I journeyed through not so long ago. Can I do it? I sense something familiar, and uneasy begin to rise in my throat, the tiniest whisper of Panic. No, I think, not again! Haven't I passed through enough mountains? Haven't I already stumbled through the darkest valleys? The grass stirs at my feet as You cradle my face in Your scarred hands.

You bend Your mouth to my ear, and You whisper, "You are stronger than you think, beloved. I AM here." The scent of Your breath revives my soul, and fear is pushed away. The sight of Your Staff brings me comfort. Didn't it beat back the brambles and reveal paths where there seemed to be none? Did it not stave off the enemy's fatal blows as I passed through that last valley? And was it not there, always before me, as You led me around that mountain and parted the waters that threatened to engulf me? Yes, yes it was, and yes, yes, You were.

With renewed hope and remembered faith, I turn to face the path You've laid out before me. You are already walking, and I hurry to catch up to You. The beauty we pass as we walk side by side along this wide, easy path is breathtaking. The sights, scents, and sounds are water to my soul, and each grows stronger as You pass by, as if they know their Maker is in their midst. Joy!

We travel in comfortable silence for a good distance before You stop, looking beyond the mountains. I follow Your gaze to the snapping banner, past the last looming mountain. I look at You. You're smiling. You are beautiful. Laughter rolls from Your lips, and You turn to me. "Wait 'til you get there," You say.

Time passes too quickly in this place of beauty, and soon the wildflowers begin to fade away, and I notice small rocks have replaced the quiet swish of the grass underfoot. The path narrows a bit, and the footing is less sure. I am paying more attention to the growing size of the rocks than to my surroundings and Your presence. Unpleasant memories of what happened last time I became distracted flood my mind. "Stay alert and focus on the Staff," I chide myself. "Remember what you were taught." I am not alone, and I am not forsaken. He makes a way when there seems to be none…remember…remember…

You are up ahead, walking with confidence and silent strength. I watch as Your Staff easily moves larger rocks and thorny bushes out of my way. You are not worried or concerned. You have my destination in mind, and You will not be swayed or deterred. Days go by as we walk this new path of rocks and brush, gnarled roots jutting up just enough to pose hazardous to my tired feet. I stumble frequently, and You patiently stop and help me up each time. Soon the sun dips out of sight, and night falls. The going is getting harder now, and I tire more easily. Sleep comes quickly as I lie down near You. I rest in Your peace. As I drift off to sleep, my mind is soothed and quieted, as the fears and worries of the day's journey are eclipsed by the sound of You singing over me as I rest. I have never heard a lovelier sound. Heaven.

In the light of morning, I take in our surroundings. Today we start up the first of the mountains, having traveled over the hills for a while now. I'm not looking forward to this part of the trip. I have grown comfortable in the hills, and I remember what the mountains of the past held. The path is steeper and much narrower. Not that far ahead, the path winds and twists out of sight, and I cannot see ahead. Fear slowly and stealthily attaches itself to me, and I do not follow You as quickly or as closely as at the start of our journey.

I hear noises that frighten me as I pick my way up the path. Shadows flicker and slink in the dark shade of the boulders that line my path. Panic joins Fear, and my thoughts get muddled as their voices mock me.

"You are out of control," they tease.

"You'd better make your own way; You are alone."

"This way is much faster," they reason smoothly.

"Go ahead and try it; you may just beat Him there."

"Yes," I say. "No harm in taking an easier route. I'll plan it out myself; no sense in getting too tired and sore climbing over and sliding about on this slick, unknown path. This path over here looks well-worn and safe."

Panic and Fear retreat a little, and Arrogance moves up to whisper in my ear, "You can do this, no problem. You can teach others how to navigate these mountains. Show them the shortcuts. You'll be a pro."

The well-worn path veers sharply to the left, and I march on with renewed self-importance. I can get there quicker, and it will save so much time and effort. How smooth and easy this new path is, why would anyone take that twisting and unknown one I was traveling? Briefly, an image of the brilliant banner flashes through my mind, but Arrogance and Self Reliance quickly distract me with a tantalizing reminder that I am in control now.

Pleased with myself, I continue down this wider path, lost in my self-serving thoughts. I notice it's getting hard to breathe. It seems stuffy and stale, suffocating. The lightly fragranced breeze that was tousling my hair and buoying me onward has died away, and it's very still. A bitter, pungent smell begins to filter through the still air. There is a distinct odor of decay and loss. This seems too familiar. I see the white glint of bones in the shadowy darkness descending around me. This path is wider but filled with death. No! No! I know this place; I know it. I know it, and I am terrified of it; wasn't I just here?

Panic rushes forward, and I cannot think clearly. Fear and Dismay dance and leap around me, shrieking, laughing, knocking me down, convincing me I'm stuck, that there is no way out. I huddle alone on the ground, visions of a brightly colored banner streaming through my mind. If only I could get to it. Before the wet heaviness of despair fully falls, the faint sound of the sure and steady tread of familiar feet catches my attention. A glimpse of something solid and safe comes slowly into view.

It comes closer and stops above my head; the taunting jeers end. I look up and see You standing above me, the Staff in Your hand. The eyes I see looking down at me are filled with compassion and something deeper I can't name, yet I respond to it willingly, feeling my parched throat soften and my ease of breathing return. I feel the sweet release, as what were the beginnings of chains clatter to the ground. You lift me up and carry me. As You take me through this deep, dark valley of shadows and death, I fear no evil. The mocking voices are silenced, the stench of death is overridden by the breath of Life.

There are more days of arduous travel left, yet Your Staff comforts me. There are more mountains to conquer, valleys to endure, storms to weather, and paths to be revealed. There are times when You go before me to show me the path and make my way clear, yet You are also behind me, hemming me in. My Protector. At other times, You walk by my side, Your hand resting gently, yet possessively on my shoulder. I am safe because I belong to You. I am Yours, and no words can describe what that knowledge does for my soul. Knowing my every thought and points of weakness, You speak out words of encouragement when snippets of mocking laughter or menacing shadows threaten to overwhelm or distract me. Fear, Panic, Dismay, and Arrogance have no place here. Prophesy flows out from Your mouth as You shout over me Your plans, Your vision, my destiny. It is more than I can take in; my thoughts are not Your thoughts, but Your Spirit captures those declarations and plants them deep in my soul, to be watered by my tears and looked after by Your very words which will not return to You void.

As I struggle on the slippery rocks of a steep slope, my fingers scrabbling for a handhold, You reach out Your right hand to me and pull me up over a craggy outcropping of rock. As You settle my feet on the ground, I see that the path is once again soft and smooth, caressing my feet after the pain and sharpness of the rocky trail. Ah, what a blessing.

"What do you see?" You breathe in my ear. "Look around, listen, and look."

My eyes and ears are met by the vivid colors of the snapping banner. A steady, fragrant breeze billows it out and in, out and in. The colors are rich, deep, mesmerizing, colors of royalty, purity, and power. I can't look away. There is safety here. I never want to leave. I look to You, and You throw back Your head, smiling and laughing! The sound is beautiful and untamed as it ripples out and out, echoing off the mountains, resounding through the trees. Joy fills my heart just hearing it.

"Keep looking, Daughter," You shout, "I've only just begun!"

I scan the path ahead and notice a large open space. In it is a lavish table, set with the finest of dishes, glinting gold and silver with brilliant blue and brightest white. This is what I saw glittering near the banner at the start of this journey. You had already planned it and set it out for me? You prepared it for me and me alone? The magnitude of Your love descends and envelopes me. I weep without shame before You, completely captured by Your perfect, unconditional love. This is what I have been searching for in vain on those wide, well-worn paths, straying far from the narrow, uncertain one that You urged me to follow. I thought I could find it on my own. I thought I could control and command it. All along, You were leading me to it, in Your way, in Your time. I see it now.

On this table is the most sumptuous feast I have ever seen. Fruit ripened to perfection is strewn in perfect chaos around the table. Delicacies I have never encountered before are placed before me, and You gesture, I should eat. I do, and I taste Your goodness, faithfulness, patience, and generosity in every bite. In the middle of this beautiful table is a pure white marble fountain. The purest, clearest water bubbles up from its center. The water never stops flowing. Its source originates from the right hand of Your seat. Mercy. My cup runs over.

Every good and perfect gift does come from You. I have tasted it, and I have known it. I dine with You in the presence of my enemies. Fear, Arrogance, and Abuse; Rage, Pain, and Bitterness. They are there, watching from the paths I didn't take, peeking from the thorny bushes that pricked me and drew blood. They taste defeat, while I taste victory, freedom, and deliverance.

As we dine together, you rise and stand next to me, raising a golden horn of oil above me. You anoint my head. I am chosen, wanted, redeemed, and purified in Your sight. You set Your seal upon me and pour out Your blessing over me.

"You have an open invitation at this table, child, do you not know? How long I have waited for you to come and dine with Me! Dwell here in My house all the days of your life. My goodness and love will follow you; watch for them, listen. Keep your eyes on My banner; never let it out of your sight."

His banner over me is love.

Acknowledgements

Writing this book has been a crazy and exciting adventure! I am eternally grateful for the outpouring of support and prayers from so many people in my sphere.

I want to thank my parents, Mike and Nancy Anderson, for being my biggest cheerleaders. From the get-go, you encouraged me to publish my writing, put myself out there and see what God does. You believed in me. Your support, prayers, and advice are priceless. I will never forget it!

To my amazing husband and kids – Paul, Emma, and Josh Giomi – thank you for being excited for me and encouraging me to go for it and get this book published! You mean the world to me!

My dear friends, Wendy Moon and Tina Harrell – thank you for walking with me through this journey from my blog to my book and all the in-between. Your faithful prayers, friendship, heartfelt joy, and excitement for my book blessed me and touched my heart. You are treasures!

Most of all, I am humbled and honored that God made a way for this book to come to fruition. He opened doors, whispered encouragement, and provided the discernment and inspiration for the words He gave me to write and send forth. From His heart to my pen...

Author bio

Melissa Giomi is a Northern California native, born in Redding. She lives near San Francisco with her husband, Paul, and their pets. They have two adult children.

Melissa is passionate about Jesus, nature, books, and good coffee. She can be found puttering in the garden and spending early mornings on the patio. She and her husband enjoy relaxing by the ocean or hiking and camping in the Redwoods.

Actively seeking joy, hope and healing on her journey through breast cancer, Melissa discovered that divine encounters happen everywhere that eyes, ears, and hearts are open.